MW01233439

# Love, Life, & Fairytale

## VICKIE VALLADARES

ISBN 978-1-63525-141-8 (Paperback)
ISBN 978-1-68197-831-4 (Hard Cover)
ISBN 978-1-68197-830-7 (Digital)

Copyright © 2016 by Vickie Valladares

All rights reserved. No part of this publication may be reproduced, distributed, or transmitted in any form or by any means, including photocopying, recording, or other electronic or mechanical methods without the prior written permission of the publisher. For permission requests, solicit the publisher via the address below.

Christian Faith Publishing, Inc.
296 Chestnut Street
Meadville, PA 16335
www.christianfaithpublishing.com

Printed in the United States of America

To the memory of my mother, Marcia D. Valladares

You were a constant support in everything I did. I'm sorry you couldn't see the finished product, but I hope I've made you proud.

# *Acknowledgments*

Thanking God is a given. Without Him, none of this would have been possible. Without His occasional whisperings of finishing what I started, I doubt I would have continued this writing process. He deserves all the praise and glory, and I am thankful that He has given me the gift of writing; it truly has helped me in my darkest hours.

I would also like to thank my mom, who has passed away. She encouraged me in everything, and she never went a day without telling me how proud she was of me. I miss you dearly, and I hope I continue to make you proud.

Next, my husband, the one whom my soul loveth! Thank you for all of your love, patience, and support. Thank you for sharing me with all my characters and their issues. I love you, babe! My wonderful mother-in-law, what can I say, you are the best!

To my dad and Nora, you both have been such a constant support in my life and have taught me the values I need to be the woman God created me to be. I love you both so much and could not have made it this far without you.

To my pastor and his family, you didn't have to help me as much as you did, and I will be forever grateful for all the time you dedicated into this project. Evangelist Rhonda Simmons, my mother in the Lord and English teacher extraordinaire, thank you so much for all of your help, time, and constructive criticism.

This book wouldn't be possible without all those mentioned. This is truly a dream come true, and I feel so blessed to have those I love help make this dream a reality.

# Preface

It was February 2008. I was a senior in high school, living in a small town in rural Mississippi. As I was driving through town, I realized many couples were preparing to celebrate Valentine's Day in church. The preachers would preach about the true love of Christ. *If I were a preacher,* I thought, *what would I preach about? Love is a given.* But love to me seemed so cliché. Everyone my age was tossing the word around like a soccer ball. "I would speak of the love of Christ, but I would also talk about life and how life can harden our hearts, making it hard for us to let a loving God in. But I also want to talk to those who believe that the love of God is a fairy tale." And that's when I got an idea to do a three-part series called "Love, Life, and Fairy Tale." I drove home and began to write.

In my church, many times before the service, a skit would be presented as an aide to the preaching. From there, I thought of my characters and wrote out the beginning of their stories. When I finished, I told my mom about my three-part series idea and how each series would begin with a skit. She read the skit and said, "Forget the series! I want to see what happens to these people! Finish the stories!"

On November 23, 2008, my mother passed away from lung disease. I remember standing outside, clutching my composite notebooks that held my stories. In front of me was a pit in which we had started a fire. Feeling hopeless, I held out the notebooks with every intention of throwing them into the crackling fire. What was the point of moving forward if my mom wouldn't be here to see how the story ends? She encouraged me to follow my dreams; she encouraged me to write and to do the things that God called me to do, but how could I without my mom? Turning away from the fire, I braced myself to drop the notebooks. I loosened my grip and then felt a voice from deep within me. It travailed, "Stop! Don't." I immediately hugged the notebooks close to my chest got on my knees and cried.

After my mother's passing, I moved to Texas with my father. I found a wonderful church that fed me the unadulterated word of God. After some months, I felt the urge to write again. Finishing the story was such a bittersweet feeling. I couldn't show it off to my mom who was so supportive, but at the same time, I knew she would be proud that I finished it. I pray this book encourages you and brings you a deeper understanding to the love of God, the life in which He has blessed us with, and the truth of His word.

In Christ,
Vickie Valladares

# *Love*

Carole-Anne wanted nothing more than his happiness. But what she wanted even more was to be a part of his happiness. As Carole-Anne watched the man of her dreams kiss his overprivileged fiancée, she couldn't help but smile at the thought of pulling the woman by the hair and taking her place in the loving kiss.

"Oh Jesus, help me," Carole-Anne said as she laughed at herself. She shook her head and chuckled. She knew God was behind this torture. Of all the cafés in Chicago, they would choose this particular café to enjoy a latte. *Laugh it up, God,* she thought.

Carole-Anne tried to focus on the deliciousness of her chamomile tea but nearly dropped her cup when she heard the most wonderful thing—his laugh. Carole-Anne's heart began to beat rapidly, and her head began to rush with envious thoughts. *I could make him laugh like that,* she thought. Carole-Anne placed her tea cup on a little saucer and stared at her blueberry muffin, which seemed massive on the napkin. She ignored the slight rumbling of her stomach and turned her gaze toward the happy couple who sat just ten feet away. But did he notice her? Did he study her like she studied him? Why couldn't she have this man? She loved him from the moment she laid eyes on him. Why did he have to be engaged? Why couldn't she be engaged to him instead of that...

Carole-Anne took another sip of her tea to calm her nerves. Here she was, shaking and getting upset over a man who was ten feet away who didn't even notice she was there. And did he notice? Of course not! He was far too busy laughing and being lovey-dovey with his fiancée. They might as well have been on different planets!

Carole-Anne took a rather large bite of her muffin in frustration, and then the feeling in her stomach turned, making her almost queasy. It was the feeling that she was being watched. She instantly looked up and caught the blue-green eyes of the very man she had been admiring from afar. She froze.

His fiancée turned and saw her and smiled warmly and waved. Carole-Anne smiled lightly and raised her tea cup in acknowledgement to the couple. She pretended to take a sip and was outraged when she realized she was trembling. She, more forcefully than intended, slammed her tea cup down, making quite a ruckus that startled her and the people who sat near her. Carole-Anne sighed and rubbed her forehead. Frustrated, she tore a piece of her muffin and shoved it in her mouth. Glancing up again, she was startled to see that the couple was gone.

Carole-Anne swallowed the muffin and was startled by the harshness of the muffin going down her throat and then realized she'd forgotten to chew it. She gulped down the rest of her tea and walked quickly out of the café. She'd hoped that she could at least get one last look at the man she thought was the love of her life.

# *Life*

Paul Rivers made his last purchases in the market. The crowds in the marketplace of downtown Chicago had caused him a slight headache. He now regretted taking his daughter, Michelle, to accompany him. She was a bundle of curiosity and loved very much to be the center of attention. He had to keep his eyes open at all times. For one second, Michelle was beside him, and the next, she was gone and nowhere to be found. Paul was not a man who gave way to his anger or frustrations. His children rarely ever saw him angry, and they wanted to keep it that way.

"Michelle," he called her attention from a homeless woman who sold flowers on the curb of the market.

"Daddy!" Michelle came running with her bright brown eyes shining. "She has pretty flowers, Daddy! Can we buy a flower for Mama?"

"Oh, Michelle—"

"Please, Daddy. Mama would love it! They're so pretty. Please." Michelle's eyes glistened in her pleading, which never failed to tug on Paul's heartstrings.

"All right, but only if you give your daddy a kiss and tell him that you love him." Paul smiled.

Michelle smiled brightly and jumped on her father. Paul dropped his bags and lifted Michelle up to his cheek where Michelle kissed him loudly. "I love you, Daddy."

Paul sighed as his heart turned to liquid in his chest. "I love you too, Michelle."

He placed Michelle down and dug in his pockets for change.

"Go on, give this to the lady and pick a flower for your mother."

Paul watched, smiling, as his daughter made the purchase. How he loved that little girl. Paul has three children. David, the eldest, is ten, and the twins, Michael and Michelle are 5. He loved all his children, but he had to admit, there was something about those bright brown eyes and her dark curly brown hair that made his life so full of joy and light. Michelle was daddy's little girl.

Michelle returned with four white roses that were wrapped in aluminum.

"Aren't they pretty, Daddy? Will Mommy like them?" she asked.

Paul smiled. "She will love them."

Paul picked up the grocery bags and grunted, "You gonna help your daddy carry the bags home?"

Michelle gleamed, "Oh yes! I can help you 'cuz I'm a strong girl, see!" Michelle pumped out her chest and raised her arm and flexed.

"Oh wow!" Paul exclaimed. "Well, since you're so strong, I might make you carry me home."

Michelle's eyes lit up with delight and mischief.

"I can't carry you, Daddy!" she said with an innocence that took Paul's very breath away.

"Why not?" Paul asked in a shocked tone.

"Cuz you're too fat!" Michelle said, poking his belly.

"Hey!" Paul laughed as he neared close to Michelle. Michelle giggled and ran into the parking lot of the market.

"Hey, Michelle, don't run! Michelle!" Paul ran after his daughter. "Michelle, stop!" Paul yelled, which was followed by the distant giggling of his daughter.

"Chase me, Daddy!" Michelle darted in between parked cars out of sight from her father.

"Michelle, stop!" Paul dropped his grocery bags and ran in between cars.

"Michelle!" Paul yelled frantically.

"Come chase me!" said the faint voice. Paul stopped and paced his breathing. Panic had set in, causing him to be short of breath. Some feet away, he noticed a couple who were staring at him. Paul ran over to them. "Excuse me, I'm sorry, I've lost my daughter. Maybe, you've seen her? She's five years old, has long brown hair, and wearing a jean skirt. Please, have you seen her?"

The couple shook their head and apologized. A sob broke out from Paul's throat. His heart pounded in his chest, and his blood raced through his veins. And in an instant, his heart stopped, his blood ran cold, and chills went through his body. First came the bone-chilling scream, screeching tires, and a loud thump that seemed to shake the ground.

Paul turned to find a crowd gathering in one side of the parking lot. People had begun to shout, and a woman began screaming.

"Oh God, oh God," was all Paul could muster as he ran toward the crowd. Desperate to get through, he clawed, ripped, and pushed his way through the crowd. Finally, he had seen what caused the crowd to gather. Paul fell to his knees and fought the rise of sickness that threatened him. The car had a dent on the front, stained with blood, and a small figure that lay just under the hood. He strained to see beyond the people who crowded the car. From under the car was pulled a little girl with long curly brown hair and whose hand gripped four white roses that were stained with blood.

"Oh, Michelle! No!"

# Fairy Tale

Leila sat hugging her knees to her chest and rocked back and forth. The chaos going on downstairs made her incredibly nervous. She wanted to do something, but what could she do? She was only ten years old! She felt so helpless and small hiding in her closet, but what else could she do? Her mother had told her to hide.

"Crouch down low, and don't make a sound!" her mother told Leila just minutes before. "No matter what happens, no matter what you hear, don't come out!" Leila wanted to argue, but her mother had fled downstairs before she could.

The yelling and chaos had seemed to get worse with every second that had passed. Leila covered her ears and tried to think of better times—times where she and her mother ran and played and talked without fear. She remembered the day when her mother took her to the park for the first time when she was eight years old. She remembered rolling down hills and the delight of feeling the grass on her skin. They chased each other. They laughed and had no worries of being too loud or too silly. This was the first time she had ever seen her mother completely loose and fun.

Leila remembered how they laid out on the blanket in the park, looking up at the clouds. Everything seemed so normal and fun. And yet Leila knew this would not last.

"Mama, what do you do when you're scared?" Leila asked, still looking up at the clouds.

With a sigh, Leila's mother rolled on her side to face her daughter. "I talk to Jesus."

Leila frowned. "Who's Jesus?"

"Jesus is the only one in the whole world who loves you more than me."

"More than you? Well, how come I've never met him?"

"Well, he's everywhere. He's in the air that we breathe. He's the water that we drink. We may never know what He looks like, but He knows us by heart. There's a whole book about Him."

"There is?"

"Yes, it's called the Bible. And it tells how the whole world came to exist, how you and I came to exist. It tells the story of Jehovah God and how He came down to Earth thousands and thousands of years ago to be a living a sacrifice for us."

Leila stared at her mother and finally said the first thing that came to her mind, "Huh?"

Leila's mother laughed, but behind her dark eyes laid an urgency, an urgency to share her faith with her daughter. She knew that this would be the only opportunity to do so.

And to help Leila understand, she started from the beginning— with the creation of the world, the creation of man and woman and how their disobedience caused them to hide from God. She spoke of Cain and Abel, Moses and the Israelites, Noah and the great flood, Jonah and the fish, Ezekiel and Jeremiah—every detail of the Old Testament that she could remember.

And finally, she came to the story of Jesus. Leila hung onto every word her mother spoke. Her mother had told her stories before, but none with as much passion and wonder as she did these stories.

She awed at the magnificence of it—men walking on water, healing the sick and the blind, turning water into wine.

"He was a magician!" Leila exclaimed.

Her mother couldn't help but burst into laughter. "No, no, Leila. He was God! God manifested himself as man. Jesus is God in flesh."

"Wow!" Leila said completely amazed.

"Yes, God had come to free His people from sin and to give them new hope of a greater, more real relationship with Him. But the teachers and priests did not believe Him. They thought He was a liar and a false prophet. They not only thought He was crazy, but also evil too."

"No way! How could an evil person heal the sick or the blind?" Leila said angrily.

"They thought He did this with the help of demons."

Leila scoffed, "Well what did Jesus do about it?"

"He continued doing miracles and preaching sermons, but one night, one of his followers betrayed him. His name was Judas, and Judas went to the priests, and for thirty silver coins, he told the priests where to find Jesus so that they could kill him."

Leila gasped.

"Jesus was tried, beaten, and tortured nearly to death and nailed on a cross to die."

"Oh no."

"Yes, but the night He was captured, He told his disciples that three days after His death, He would rise again. And guess what?"

"What?" Leila said, inching closer to her mother.

"He did! And then He went to heaven on a cloud. And gave us his Holy Spirit to dwell among us. And there was one particular day, called the day of Pentecost, when his disciples and family all gathered together in the upper room. And all were filled with the Holy Ghost. They spoke in tongues and were baptized in Jesus's name."

"Holy Ghost, tongues? I don't get it," Leila said, shaking her head.

"The Holy Ghost is the spirit of God. It's His gift to us. It's His way of being with us always. And speaking in tongues is a sign of that gift. It's when you speak in a language that you don't understand."

Leila sighed, "I'm confused."

"It's a way of talking to God. It's a way to know that His spirit dwells within you. Jesus wants us to talk to Him like you would talk to me. The Bible says He's closer than a friend, mother, or brother. When we pray, He hears us. He hears us even if we don't say anything out loud. All we have to do is call His name. What's His name, Leila?"

"Jesus?"

Leila's mother sighed and smiled. "Any time you feel afraid, you just say the name of Jesus. And he'll hear you. He'll protect you."

Leila was brought back from her memory as a bang rang through the air. It was so loud, what could it have been? It echoed through the entire house and made her ears ring.

Leila sat in silence trying to calm her beating heart. And then she realized after that terrifying bang, the house was completely still. Her mother's screams no longer pierced the air; the clanking and banging stopped. The house was silent as the grave. The thought sent chills throughout her body. Her heart sounded like a drum against the silence, and her breathing became like violent winds.

She wanted to run, but where could she go? She wanted her mother; she wanted to take her mother and run far away, but her mother was downstairs with *him*. Leila tried to steady her breathing, but it rose again as she heard rapid footsteps making their way up the stairs.

*Momma!* she thought but then realized as the footsteps came closer, they were too heavy to be her mother's.

Leila began to panic and hid herself behind her clothes.

"Oh Jesus, please," she prayed in state of panic.

The footsteps came in her bedroom. The door slammed open. Leila screamed then covered her mouth.

"Oh Jesus, Jesus please!" she whispered. Her closet door then swung open, and there he was. The dark figure moved the clothes aside to see Leila hugging her knees and weeping, muttering a name over and over again.

Leila could smell the strong odor of whiskey. He held a glistening object in his hand, and her face paled at the sight of it. The silver pistol was dauntingly aimed at her.

"Daddy, please," she whispered. She looked up at her father. The darkness that lingered in his eyes seemed inhuman, almost animallike. His face was flushed, and tears ran down his face. He held the pistol in place and looked at his daughter in anguish.

"I love you, Leila," he said painfully and then pulled the trigger.

# *Love*

Carole-Anne sat at her kitchen table, which was covered with books and notes. She sighed over her books and debated which lesson to teach the youth this coming Sunday. She had been teaching the Sunday-school youth class now for two years, and her lessons, sadly, were beginning to sound the same, at least to her. Something was lacking. She frowned over her studies.

To her relief, her phone began to ring, giving her a reason to take a break from her lessons. She rose to answer the phone, but of course, it wasn't where it should've been—on the charger. The phone continued ringing as she scrimmaged through the living room and finally found the phone under a pillow on the couch. Winded, she answered the phone. "Hello?" she said cheerfully.

"Well, aren't you supposed to be workin' on your Sunday-school lesson?" said the Southern voice cheerfully.

"Well, I would if someone wouldn't interrupt me," Carol-Anne said, smiling.

"Well excuse me, Ms. Comeback"—the voice laughed—"I was just callin' to check up on ya after that embarrassing display at the café today."

Carole-Anne went still. "Wh-what?'

"Mm-hmm girl, first off, I find it very rude that you did not invite me, you're best friend in the entire world, to the café with you. I like muffins too, ya know!" she rambled.

"Molly, Molly, back up, you saw?"

"Yes, ma'am, I saw you! I was passin' the café when I saw you wide-eyed and blushin'. And who do I see sittin' just ten feet away?

18

Mr. Fabulous himself and his bride-to-be. 'Poor Carole-Anne,' I thought at first, but then I stopped feelin' sorry for ya and felt angry instead. I mean, it serves you right for not invitin' me to join you!"

"Oh Molly, seriously! Why didn't you just come in and sit with me?" Carole-Anne said as the heat rose to her cheeks.

"Because I was enjoyin' the show! And then who could resist the marvelous scene when you hightailed it out of the café and followed them down the street?" Carole-Anne heard her friend clapping on the other end. "Bravo! Oh it nearly 'bout ripped my heart out!" Molly said, sniffling.

"Okay, Molly. Okay, thank you, I'm completely pathetic. Thank you for bringing it to my attention. Now if you don't mind, I'm going to hide under my bed in the fetal position and cry."

"Tsk, tsk. Carole-Anne, honey, we've been friends a long time, haven't we?" Molly asked, now wholeheartedly concerned.

"Too long," Carole-Anne said sarcastically.

"Well, girl, what were you thinkin'?"

"I don't know, Moll. I just...I don't know what I was thinking." She sighed in defeat.

"Carole-Anne, I know you think you love him, but stalkin' him isn't exactly a good way to get his attention."

"I was not stalking! I was observing from a reasonable distance," Carole-Anne said, trying to control her rising temper.

"Don't get all upset, Carole-Anne. It's just you're my best friend, and I don't want you to get hurt. It's time to face facts. He's engaged—"

"You don't think I know that, Moll!" Carole-Anne yelled. "I tell myself that every time I see him. Every time I think about him I remind myself that he's getting married. But, Moll"—Carole-Anne sighed, wiping the tears that escaped her eyes—"I love him. And I don't know what to do about it, and you laughing about it isn't helping, all right?"

Molly remained silent. The awkward silence added to Carole-Anne's frustrations. "I've got to get back to my lessons. I'll see you on Sunday."

"I love ya, girl," Molly said before Carole-Anne hung up.

"I love you too, Molly. Bye."

Carole-Anne hung up her phone and threw it on the couch and then threw herself on the couch and cried. Letting out her emotions, she returned to the table and tried to focus on her lessons. But her mind was racing in different directions. Carole-Anne couldn't help but feel guilty about being angry with Molly. She hadn't meant to yell, but she knew that was her only defense when she felt trapped—get angry and fight. But it wasn't Molly's fault that she caught her in an embarrassing act of desperate love.

"God, I'm so stupid!" she said as she slammed her fists on the table. Tears welled up in Carole-Anne's eyes, and she fought to swallow the lump that formed in her throat.

*Tap. Tap. Tap.* The tapping on the door startled her.

*Tap. Tap. Tap.* She wiped her face and made sure she was presentable. She wasn't expecting anyone. It's probably Molly coming to apologize and raid her fridge.

She opened the door and said, "Molly, you didn't have to...oh." She froze when she looked at her guest and chuckled. "You're not Molly."

Her guest smiled, which melted her heart. "Hello, Carole-Anne," he said coolly. Carole-Anne stood frozen at her doorway, unable to utter a sound.

# *Life*

Paul sat in the family room as his wife put the two boys to bed. He began to think of the boys. His beautiful boys. David favored his mother, and Michael, Paul winced. How long has it been since he looked at Michael? Not long enough, for his face still came clearly to his mind. Michael was Michelle's twin, and their faces were almost exactly alike. Since Michelle's death, Paul had not been able to look at his son. He reached over to the coffee table and grabbed the whiskey bottle and chugged.

Upstairs, after the story was read, the boys easily went to sleep. Katie sighed in relief and began to pick up the clothes and toys that were left on the floor and put everything in its proper place. Finally, she made her way downstairs. She had the wonderful idea to sit on the couch and prop her feet on the coffee table and relax. Coming down the stairs, she saw Paul had beaten her to it, but it was all right. She felt like cuddling tonight. Exhausted and weary, she sat next to her husband and leaned her head on his shoulder but quickly drew away. He reeked of alcohol. She then noticed the half-empty bottle of whiskey on his lap. She sighed and rubbed her temples.

"I thought you quit," she said, hurtful.

"I lied," Paul slurred.

Katie looked at her husband and fought the urge to push him out of the door and out of her and her boys' lives forever. Katie felt so helpless. Her husband was slipping away before her eyes, and nothing she has done or said was bringing him back. Katie sobbed as she watched her husband grab the bottle and drink deeply.

"You've had enough, Paul!" Though Katie said it quietly, her despair was clear in her face and in her voice. Paul continued to drink without acknowledging her. That felt like a slap in the face to Katie, and she looked away as the anger boiled inside. She wanted to slap him, shake him, and punch him. Anything to get his attention, but it would do no good. He was slipping away from her, perhaps quicker if she had become violent with him.

Katie looked at her husband. She loved him deeply. She didn't understand why, but as each day went by, she loved him more and more. He had given her everything. By God's grace, they were blessed with three beautiful children, a home that was fully paid for, and a fair living that they were both comfortable with. God had surely been good to them. She loved Paul with everything that was in her. She had once thought that their love for each other would pull them through any situation. No matter what they faced, they could face it together. They did everything together, went to church together, prayed together, fasted together, and were even baptized together. But now, things were different. Paul no longer depended on his wife. He had chosen not to depend on Katie's love or the Lord's. Paul, instead, depended on liquor, which made Katie feel inadequate, like her love was not enough. She was failing him. She believed that her love would sustain him like his love sustained her; perhaps, she didn't love him enough.

"Paul," she said, placing her hand on his clammy hand, "I know that you're hurting. But I'm hurting too. She was my daughter too!" Katie's voice cracked with emotion, and the tears spilled from her eyes.

"Won't you speak to me please? You still have a family that needs you. Our boys need you. I need you." Katie sobbed and knelt in front of her husband, laying her head on his lap. "You have a wife, Paul. I need you. Please, come back to me." Katie sobbed uncontrollably.

Paul sat, too drunk to understand what Katie was going on about, too drunk to care. All he knew was that her ramblings were rubbing on a nerve and making his head ache. Paul rose from his seat, grabbed his bottle, and slowly walked up the stairs to his bedroom, muttering the entire way.

Katie sat still on the floor, trembling and holding in a scream of despair. She wanted to throw a tantrum. She wanted to scream, cry, and tear at anything that was near. She could see herself tearing her house to pieces, breaking everything in sight. She wanted to so badly. The rage and grief rose inside of her, causing her head to pound. She trembled and cried so hard it took her breath away.

Lying down on the floor, she began to think of her Michelle, of the day she passed away, and she thought of the strain it had caused her family. David never dealt with it; Michael hasn't spoken a single word since her death; and Paul...Paul. Too weary to cry anymore, Katie rose from her spot on the floor and made her way upstairs. Before going to bed, she made it a habit to check on her children. The boys were tucked soundly in their beds. Those two were a handful and stressed her to the point that she wanted to pull her hair out and sometimes theirs. David was always picking on Michael, and Michael was always taking David's toys. Though Michael never spoke, he was still very mischievous. Michael never played since Michelle's death. No matter how hard Katie and David pushed him, he never played. But on occasion, he would hide David's toys and smile slyly while David went crazy looking for his action figure.

Katie smiled and held in a laugh. She knew Michael hiding David's toys was Michael's way of coming back. She often had to remind David not to get too angry with his brother. That was his brother's way of playing. She next, out of habit, went to Michelle's room. She knew Michelle would not be there, but it made her feel better to know everything was where it should be. She had left her room exactly how it was before she passed away. The walls were painted pink with a lime-green trim. Her dolls were still scattered on the floor. Her closet door always remained closed to prevent the monsters from coming into her room. Her princess castle night light protected her from darkness, and a picture of her mom and dad still stood on her nightstand, keeping watch.

Katie sighed. "You're watching over us now, Michelle."

Katie walked over to her bedroom and was bombarded with the smell of liquor. She looked at her husband who was sprawled across the bed snoring lightly. And the bottle of whiskey had been spilled all over her satin bedsheets. Katie fought the urge to yank him out of bed and pour the remaining alcohol in his face and then frowned when she realized that what was left of it was soaking in her bedsheets. She mourned her ruined sheets and looked at the man responsible. She was so weary of him. She studied the man she called her husband and searched within to find the love that weighed in her heart. But all she felt for him was pity. Katie shook her head and closed the door behind her.

# *Fairy Tale*

The door was closed behind her. The job had been done. It was over, at least for now. Leila sighed, not in satisfaction of a job well done, rather in sorrow. She knew down deep in her soul this would never be over. There would always be more men, and the shadows that haunted her would continue to torment. Eight years had passed since her father, in a drunken rage, killed her mother and then, in front of her, killed himself. Eight long hard years had passed, and with each year, the torment that it left behind became heavier and heavier. Added to the weight of her past was the weight of the life she had been living. She had been trained to be desired, to be loved for an hour. Men looked at her and saw beauty, but she saw a dirty, unloved, useless toy to be passed around from person to person. This was her life; it was all she had and all she knew, and inside, she was breaking. Tears began to sting the back of her eyes as she leaned on the door she had closed behind her. She was drowning, and no one would pull her up. Angry, she straightened, wiped the tears from her eyes, and walked out of the run-down apartment complex and began to walk down the street. From inside her tiny purse, her cell phone rang. The contact name was Boss.

"Hello," Leila answered.

"Yo, Lil' Mama."

"Hey, Boss. I'm done with the old man."

"Yeah, I see you Lil' Mama. I'm across the street."

Leila heard the honking from across the street and saw the shiny black mustang with tinted windows.

"I'm coming," Leila said and hung up the phone. Leila walked toward the mustang and opened the door. As soon as she opened the door, smoke spilled out, and the aroma of the drug of the hour filled the air.

"You shouldn't be driving with the windows closed," Leila said, trying not to cough.

"Shut up and get in," Boss ordered.

She did as her boss told her and lowered the window so she could breathe.

"You got my money?"

"Of course." Leila reached in her purse and pulled out a wad of cash and gave it to Boss. He took the cash and stopped the car to count it.

"Good job, Lil' Mama. Here"—he handed her a small portion of it—"buy yo'self some candy." He chuckled slightly, showing off his silver grill and took another hit of the blunt in his hand.

Leila counted the amount he gave her and sighed. She deserved more for being with someone she hardly knew. But she wouldn't dare say so; her mouth always got her into trouble.

"Here, you'll need to take a hit for your next client. It'll help you relax." Boss gave her the blunt, and Leila took a hit and tried not to cough.

"Who"—Leila's head began to swim—"who's my next client?"

"Some rich fool. Lives out in the 'burbs. Came to me this mornin' looking for some fun. Said he wanted the best girl. You know who that is, huh Lil' Mama?" Boss laughed.

Leila smiled sarcastically. She hated Boss. But she knew she wouldn't have been able to make it without him. He plucked her out of the streets and invited her to live in his apartment. He kept her well fed, well dressed, and pretty much gave her run of his apartment. He gave her a home. What eighteen-year-old, working the streets could say she had her own upscale apartment?

But nothing in this world came free. Because of the financial burden Leila placed on him, she began to work for him as a call girl. She didn't live on the streets anymore; now she owned them. He paid her well and always made sure she was in shape. She helped him out by purging herself once in a while, but to make things easier on her throat, she wouldn't eat at all. He had always told her when she was getting too fat or too skinny. But she was never able to find a balance when it came to her body. Everyone thought she was beautiful. She caught the attention of every man she passed by, but all her life, she felt ugly and dirty. She could never look anyone in the eyes for fear that they could see how filthy she really was. The last person she ever looked in the eyes was her mother. And now her mother was just cloud in her memory. But Leila never dwelt on the past; it reminded her too much of her present.

"Yo, girl. Why you lookin' so serious?"

"Nothing, just thinking about my next job."

"Well, don't think on it, Lil' Mama. This dude's loaded. He sho' to pay you double what you make regularly, you know what I'm sayin'?"

"Yeah."

Leila had always felt wrong about the things she did. She had heard once that this part of her life was special. And this special side of her life is to be reserved for one special person. One person only, should she share it with. She didn't know where she had heard it from, but she knew she heard it once or twice. Shame gripped her, and a feeling of worthlessness overcame her. What she had to offer was no longer special; it was something that everyone wanted, and just about anyone could have it.

As the black mustang made its way to the high-priced suburban neighborhood, Leila began her ritual of makeup, perfume, and hair. She straightened her blouse and de-fuzzed her black jeans. She didn't believe in wearing what the other girls wore. They wore revealing clothes that were five sizes too small. She thought the look to be cheap and trashy. Perhaps, her job didn't give her much respect, but she was doing business, and she would dress like a business woman. The fact that the look made her seem older was a plus too. Leila covered her body as much as possible; she didn't flaunt, and she didn't entice. If men wanted her, then they would have her. If they didn't, well, she never complained.

"He wants two hours with you. I'll be back by then to pick you up." Leila made her way out of the car and took one last hit of Boss's blunt. Boss scanned her up and down, proud of his little money-maker. He reached over and kissed her.

"I'll see you in a few hours. Make sure you eat a mint before you go in." Leila nodded and watched as the mustang sped and turned out of the cul-de-sac.

Leila turned and saw a beautiful white columned house. Though the house was beautiful, it was lacking in homey touches. Perhaps some shrubs or flower gardens would look nice. Parked in the driveway was a silver BMW. On the back of the bumper was a fish symbol, which Leila recognized as a Christian symbol.

"Nice."

She made her way up the steps and rang the doorbell. She forced a smile but was struck with surprise as she saw the dark hair and dark eyes. This man was quite handsome in his business suit and seemed fairly young. Leila estimated him to be in his early twenties.

"Are you Leila?"

"The one and only, handsome." Leila winked.

"Chris has told me a lot about you," he said, referring to the man she knew as Boss.

"So, you're a Christian?" Leila said slyly.

"Why do you say that?" he asked wide-eyed. She looked at his car and pointed to the bumper. The young man laughed and ran his hand through his black hair.

"I'm Matthew."

Leila smiled at the man as he grabbed her hand and escorted her inside his home.

# *Love*

There he was, just staring at her. His teeth were amazingly white, and his eyes sparkled in the dim light and made Carole-Anne's knees buckle. There he was, the man of her dreams.

"Carole-Anne?"

"Oh." He made her name sound sweet like honey from his lips. Derek cleared his throat, feeling incredibly uncomfortable. Carole-Anne gasped, realizing that she had stood gawking at him.

"I'm sorry, Derek! My mind is just not here." She laughed nervously. "Um, come on in." She held the door open and lost herself again as Derek swept by, and the intoxicating aroma of his cologne enticed her senses. She stood, breathing deeply.

Derek turned to see Carole-Anne's eyes closed and her lips smiling and suddenly regretted coming here by himself. He stood impatiently and noticed how she clung to the door and sighing heavily. Derek cleared his throat to gain her attention.

Carole-Anne gasped and found that she had stood as if in a trance. She hurriedly closed the door and joined him in her living room.

"Um"—Carole-Anne chuckled—"can I get you something to drink?"

"No, no thank you." Derek smiled politely and gazed over her books.

"I won't be long. I see I interrupted your studies. I'm sorry."

"No, no don't be. I needed a break." She felt herself begin to tremble. She realized how crazy she must have seemed to him. She was slightly trembling, smiling, and chuckling. She fought incredibly for composure.

"So, um, please, take a seat," she said, pointing toward the couch.

"No, I'd rather stand," Derek said, smiling.

"Um, okay. So what's up?"

Derek raked his hand through his dirty blonde hair and sighed heavily.

"Is something wrong?" Carole-Anne asked, getting nervous.

Derek moved over to her table and pushed some of her books aside to leave room to rest his elbow.

"I just, um wanted to touch base with you, and I guess talk about your behavior," Derek said carefully.

"My behavior?" Carole-Anne said, confused.

"Yes, your behavior toward me.," Derek said, clearing his throat.

Suddenly, Carol-Anne felt cold, her hands paled and chilled. Her body froze, and her face turned hot. She felt the full force of the heat on her cheeks. She stood still while her heart raged in a beating frenzy.

"I don't understand," she said, trembling.

Carole-Anne watched as he exhaled in frustration. His eyes seemed to deepen, giving him a more exotic look. She noticed how his brows twitched slightly in his concentration. She knew she could spend her whole life just watching him, and that would make her happy. Derek Smith was a man who stole her heart from the beginning. He was a strong man, passionate, and, more importantly, he was a godly man. She saw Derek to be like David from the Bible—a man after God's own heart. He was certainly a man who had hers. How she desired to know him more, to be with him, and here he was sitting at her kitchen table. Wait, why was he here?

"Anne!" Derek shouted.

"Oh!" Carole-Anne jumped and placed her hand on her heart.

"You see! That's what I'm talking about!" Derek breathed and pushed down his uprising anger.

She felt herself getting smaller by the second. Her stomach turned, and her heart was painfully rapid.

"Please, Carole-Anne, take a seat." Derek motioned for the chair next to him. Suddenly, at the request, her humiliation turned to anger, which was her defense mechanism when she felt trapped.

"I'll stand, thank you. And who gives you the right to come in here and wave orders around like I was your child or something? Not in my home!"

"Whoa, whoa," Derek said, lifting his hands. "I didn't mean for it to sound commanding— "

"Why don't you just say what you came here to say?" she snapped.

"Fine. Fine." Derek sighed and passed his hand through his hair. "I came here personally to tell you that this infatuation you have with me has to stop. Being the youth pastor, I've been asked to assist in the Sunday-school class, which means you and I will be working together. And I don't want to have to worry about you giving me goo-goo eyes during the lessons. It's embarrassing for me and you. And the last thing I need are rumors going around and ruining the relationship with my fiancée. No, I refuse to let that happen. And if you can't control your adolescent fantasies, then I will have you removed from this ministry. I know what those kids mean to you and what you mean to those kids, but so help me, Carole-Anne, if your behavior toward me doesn't change, then you will be replaced. Is that understood?"

Carole-Anne took a seat on her couch, stunned. His voice was so stern. She felt like a disobedient child. She wanted to crawl under her bed and stay there. But this was not the time. He was in her house, sitting on her chair. She would tell him a thing or two.

"I understand. I'm sorry for all the trouble I've caused you. I didn't mean to," she said. Sickened at herself, she couldn't even look at him for the fear she would burst into tears.

Derek sighed in relief that the confrontation was over. "Let's just put it behind us. I'm looking forward to your lesson on Sunday. From the look of all your books here, it should be very good."

Derek rose and stood in front of Carole-Anne. Her face was struck with sorrow and red from embarrassment. He couldn't help but feel the pang of guilt.

"Can I ask you a question, Derek?" she said without looking at him.

"Please do."

"Why did you stop at my house to tell me this?" Derek remained silent. "Anyone else would have called a meeting with the elders of the church. Why did you come to my house?"

"Well I—"

"Was it because you wanted to see me?" she said, finally looking up at him. "If my affections for you were so adolescent, I believe you wouldn't have even bothered. Any other man would not have been so troubled. But you were. Why? Is it because maybe you're attracted to me too?" Carole-Anne said it in a faint whisper. Though Derek remained silent, the expression on his face was enough to confirm her suspicions. She stood to face him. The embarrassment had gone from her face, and her cheeks blushed, not with humiliation or anger but with love. She stood so close to him, his scent overwhelmed her. Carole-Anne inched closer. She knew if she let go, he would too. With a sigh, she closed her eyes and waited.

Derek put his hands on her shoulders and lightly nudged her aside. Without saying a word, he made his way to her front door only to pause to say one last thing, "Whatever assumptions you have about me is far from the truth. I do not and will never have feelings for you. I love my fiancée, and no one will change that. Ever."

With that, Derek exited her home.

Carole-Anne stood, sure that at any moment, her heart would stop beating, and she would die alone in her home. But her heart continued to pound, and her lungs continued breathing. Keeping her composure, she returned to the table and began reading over her guidelines. She refused to let any emotions escape. Her loneliness and pain would be hidden from the world. And her heartbreak will be quickly wiped away just like her falling tears.

# *Life*

Paul awoke to the sound of whooping and his boys laughing. On a normal day, the sound of his children at play would entice him to join along. He would scoop up his children and kiss them until they pushed him away. He would run and play until his wife had to remind him who were the children in the house. But all that seemed impossible now. Instead of wishing he could play, he wished he were dead.

The sounds of his boys running up and down the hallways made it seem like his house was filled with drums, and the drums surrounding him were growing louder and louder. The sunlight that peaked through the curtains were like lasers in eyes. He felt nauseous but had no strength to get up. Paul covered his head under the pillow and groaned. Even the sound from his own throat caused his head to pound and swirl. His boys' laughter became louder, and their footsteps pounded on the floor. He held the pillow tighter around his head and pleaded that God would kill him now.

With a bang, David and Michael barged through his bedroom door. David was dressed as a cowboy, and little Michael was dressed as an Indian.

"Dad, wake up!" David said, poking his father. "Come on, Dad, we're playing cowboys and Indians. I'm the cowboy, and Michael's an Indian. Mom's playing too. She's an Indian, and she's my prisoner, and its Michael's job to rescue her!"

David pushed on his father.

"Dad, come on." David looked at his brother Michael who had begun to drop his shoulders. David got closer to his dad and whispered, "Come play with us. It's been a long time since we all played together as a family. You should see Michael. He's playing with us. He's even laughing. Maybe today will be the day he starts talking."

Before, an hour or so of play would cure whatever ailed Paul. But not today. Not with his head pounding and his stomach turning. He wanted peace; he wanted to be left alone. To suffer alone.

"Go away," Paul said through his teeth.

"Dad—"

"David!" Paul yelled under the pillows, "I'm not in the mood. Now go away."

David sighed and knew his father would not join them in play. David turned to his little brother, "Come on, Michael, let's let Dad sleep."

David grabbed his little brother by the hand and began to walk, but Michael stood firm in his place. David looked at his brother, and his heart tore at the sight of him. He knew Michael was hurting just like his father was hurting. But Michael was getting better. Michael hadn't spoken a word since Michelle died. But today, there was something special in the air today for Michael and his family. For the first time since Michelle passed, Michael played and laughed. David wanted to cry when he first heard his little brother laugh, but big kids don't cry, so he chose to laugh with him. Yes, the tears came, but it was from laughing so hard. At least that was David's excuse. If Michael was coming back, then surely his dad could come back too. And why not today? David squeezed Michael's hand and motioned for him to stay put. David then stood by his father's bed.

His father usually smelled of cologne or aftershave, which were smells that made David feel safe and loved. But the strong smell that radiated out of his father made him sick to his stomach. But he knew he had to push through it, for Michael.

"Dad?" David whispered. His father made an inaudible sound that sounded more like a growl. "Remember how you used to say that you loved hearing us laugh. You could hear Michael laugh again." David tugged on the blankets. "Come on, Dad, come play."

Paul's irritation turned to guilt, which filled him with a fury he could not contain. With a burst and a growl, Paul leapt from his bed and raised his hand and brought it down with great force, striking David down with one hard blow.

"I told you to leave me alone! I told you to go away!" Paul struck his son again, and David crawled to escape another blow. David's vision had gone blurry, and everything sounded muffled. Michael was screaming and wailing. The sound pierced through his brain, and it helped David focus. David ran to his little brother and shielded him incase his father wanted to throw another blow.

"Take your brother out of here!" Paul said, covering his ears. Realizing that his children weren't moving, Paul grabbed them by their shirts and pushed them out of his room and slammed the door behind them. As soon as Paul slammed the door, he turned and ran to his bathroom and buried his head in the toilet. After his nausea passed, he sat with his back resting against the toilet seat. He could still hear Michael crying in the distance. Paul sobbed, realizing the first sound he had ever heard his youngest make since the passing of his twin was a scream. Paul laid his head on the floor and sobbed, even though with each sob brought a piercing pain into his head. The image of his son taking the blows and then shielding his brother from him made his heart ache. Paul cursed himself and begged that God would end his life now so that his family wouldn't have to suffer anymore.

"God help me please," was all Paul could muster and repeated those words over and over again.

Taking a break from her playtime, Katie went downstairs and made sandwiches for her and her boys. In the mood for milkshakes, Katie began to blend her special milkshakes for her boys. It was until an unusual sound stopped her. Screaming. This wasn't a playing scream or "there's a spider in my room" scream or even "I'm being tickled to death" scream. This was an "I'm in serious trouble" scream. Katie gasped and ran upstairs to see her boys holding each other in front of her bedroom door, which was shut. David was trembling, and Michael was screaming and crying. David's face was red, and his right eye began to swell massively. Katie rushed them both downstairs and tended to David's eye and calmed Michael while David shakily told his mom what happened.

Fast as lightning, Katie ran upstairs. This was the last straw. She knew exactly what she would do. She would hit him and push him out of their lives forever. She stomped her way to her bedroom and slammed the door shut behind her. *How dare he touch my children! This is it! It all ends now! Oh I'm going to*—her thoughts ended abruptly as she entered their bathroom. Lying on the floor in the fetal position was her husband who trembled and pleaded for God to help him. Tears came to her eyes as her heart ached for him. She had every intention of hitting him and yelling at him. She wanted him to hurt like he had made his family hurt. But she saw now that he already did.

"Jesus, give me strength," she whispered and could only think of one thing to do. Sitting on her nightstand was a small vile filled with anointing oil. Grabbing the bottle and holding it close to her chest, she walked over to her bathroom and stopped. For some reason, fear gripped her heart, but she couldn't let fear stop her. Taking a breath, Katie entered the bathroom and sat in front of her husband. He was still crying and pleading God to help him.

Katie said a silent prayer and placed the vile down beside her and, with a song, began to untie her husband's shoes that were left on from the night before. As she untied his shoelaces, she sang a song to calm her and her husband.

> I need thee every hour. Most gracious Lord
> No tender voice like thine can peace afford
> I need thee oh I need thee
> Every hour I need thee
> Oh bless me now my savior I come to thee
> I need thee every hour in joy or pain
> Come quickly and abide oh life is vain
> I need thee oh I need thee.
> Oh bless me now my savior, I come to thee.
> Oh bless me now my savior I come to thee.

While singing the hymn, Katie rubbed the anointed oil on Paul's feet. Her tears dropped while she sang, and Paul was sitting up, looking at Katie in disbelief. His heart melted as Katie sang. It broke when she cried, and it became whole as she poured the oil on his feet. He had begun to understand how Jesus must have felt when the woman broke her alabaster box and cried and prayed at his feet. But he was not Jesus; Paul was no savior. He was no god. He was a man who was angry with God. He walked away from God. He felt like God destroyed him, and in return, Paul destroyed his home.

It had been so long since he heard Katie sing. She had the most beautiful voice. The Lord was in her voice. Katie continued to sing. Her tears continued to fall, and her hands continued to massage the oil on Paul's feet. Katie felt the Lord's presence among them. She knew God had heard their cries and prayers. Katie began to pray over Paul and the demons that haunted and trapped him. She felt such power in her words and soon felt her husband stir. Paul felt the chills run through his body as his wife began to pray. He felt the touch of hope and peace. He knew at that moment that God was in the room and listening to Katie's prayers. He sobbed and finally broke; he began to pray along with his wife. And within minutes, there in their bathroom floor, they were filled with the Holy Ghost and speaking in a heavenly language.

# Fairy Tale

Leila sat at the window of her apartment looking out onto the streets of Chicago—the streets that she owned. Leila thought of her job, her boss who she lived with, and looking down from her window—which was thirty five feet up from the ground—imagined how it would feel to jump from the window and free herself of the meaningless life she lived in.

How she longed to live a normal teenage life instead of sharing her body with different men all the time. She wished for a home she was proud to call her own. Here, she was trapped. Boss used her whenever he pleased, beat her whenever he felt it right, and never once told her that he loved her. Of course, she didn't imagine anything better; she thought that was how all men treated their girlfriends and wives. That's how her mother was treated, so who was she to try to wish for anything different? But how she wished that just once, Boss would come in and show her some sort of affection, an affection that went beyond the bedroom, beyond flesh, and beyond lust. She wanted an affection that went through her heart and straight to her soul.

But there was no type of affection for a girl who lived the life of a prostitute. Her job was to make the men happy, take their money, and do it all over again. On her days off, she stayed in the apartment cleaning and cooking for Boss, meeting his every need and desire. This was her life. Call her crazy, but she longed for something different.

Leila cleaned, scrubbed, vacuumed, dusted, and prepared a delicious meal of toasted turkey sandwiches, and now that her chores were done, she had some time to herself and her thoughts. But her thoughts brought her to a dark place, a place of no hope and no future. Thoughts that tempted her to take that thirty-five foot jump headfirst.

The door slamming brought Leila from her dark thoughts and looked to see Boss dragging something heavy.

"Leila!" Boss yelled.

Leila sighed. She had hoped that he would be in a good mood today, but to her luck, he came home in a very bad mood.

"What?" Leila said, rolling her eyes.

"Get over here now." Boss sneered.

Leila walked over to where Boss stood still, pulling and dragging at this very large black bag.

"Shut the door!" Boss commanded. Leila shut the door and heard Boss drop the black bag that landed with a hard thump. Leila stood with her back against the door, staring horrified at the large black bag. Boss paced, cursed, and muttered to himself as beads of sweat rolled down his dark face.

Leila glanced again at the bag. It resembled the bags she had always seen in the movies—the bags that held the dead.

"Wh-what is that?" Leila stuttered.

"A bag, what's it look like?" Boss snapped.

"What's in it?" Leila said slowly.

Boss remained silent. Swallowing down her fear, Leila walked over to the bag and leaned down, grabbed a hold of the zipper, and slowly pulled it down. Escaping the small hole that Leila unzipped was a strand of bloodstained hair. Leila fell back and gasped, fighting the urge to vomit.

"What did you do?" Leila sobbed.

With a curse, Boss walked over to the bag and began kicking it.

"Stupid. Stupid, woman!" Boss yelled.

Leila rose and tried to push Boss back, but Boss pushed her on to the couch and continued to kick and curse at the lifeless body inside.

"Boss, stop it, please stop it!" Leila cried.

Boss turned and grabbed Leila's face. Leila was sobbing uncontrollably. "You shut up! Don't say a word." He pushed Leila's face, walked over to his fridge, and grabbed a beer. Leila sat shaking on the couch.

"What are you going to do?" Leila asked as calmly as she could.

"I'm going to enjoy my beer," Boss said, raising his bottle to Leila. After taking a large gulp, he motioned to the body bag. "Get rid of it."

"Excuse me?" Leila said in shock. After lighting a cigarette, Boss walked over to his coffee table, took a remote, and turned on the TV.

"I said"—he began switching channels—"get rid of it."

"N-no!" Leila yelled, rising from the couch. "This is your mess. You get rid of it!"

Boss glared at Leila, and a muscle twitched near his mouth. Cracking his neck, he said, "Don't test me, Leila. Do it."

Leila suddenly bolted to the door, but her speed was nothing compared to Boss's. He had her by the neck and slammed her against the door.

"Where you think you goin', Lil' Mama?" He clutched Leila harder, making her gasp in pain.

"I don't think you understand who you're dealin' with here, Ma. If it weren't for me, you'd be homeless on the streets eating rats. You owe me your life. You belong to me." He sneered.

Letting her go abruptly, he turned toward the couch and sat comfortably watching a basketball game, paying no mind to the body bag that lay at his feet.

Leila stood trembling with hot tears running down her face. With nothing else to do, or nowhere else to go, she walked toward the bag.

"Hold up," Boss said without looking at her. "Wait 'til it gets dark so nobody sees you."

Leila nodded and walked to her bedroom, saying not another word. Yes, she would do what Boss asked and would wait until dark. She would dump the body somewhere and run as far as her feet would take her.

# *Love*

Two days had passed since her little confrontation with Derek. And though she pretended like it never happened, it still caused her heart to race. She couldn't stop thinking about him. She knew he had feelings for her, but were his feelings the same as hers? Or did he like her because she liked him? She'd never been more confused in her life.

Carole-Anne sat picking at her salad while Molly sat in front of her, irritated.

"You know," Molly began, "I thought when you invited me out to lunch, you could...oh, I don't know, talk!"

Carole-Anne put down her fork with a clang. "I'm sorry, Moll. I just can't stop thinking about him."

Molly took a sip of her soda. "Just think about something else. Like my new shoes for example. Aren't they lovely?" Molly held out her foot showing a pair of worn-out tennis shoes.

Carole-Anne chuckled. "They're gorgeous, Moll."

"Why thank you." Molly smiled. "I paid an arm and a leg for 'em at Payless." They both laughed.

"Moll, he's interested in me, I know it!" Carole-Anne said, hitting the table.

Molly scoffed. "Carole-Anne, come on, get serious. The man is engaged. Will you just move on?"

"No!" Carole-Anne yelled, causing some people to stare. "I will not move on," she whispered. "You don't understand, Moll. I've never felt this way about anyone, ever. Why would God give me these feelings if there wasn't something special behind them? And he's interested. I still have a chance!"

Molly sighed and bit her lip. "Carole-Anne, listen to me now. I like to think of myself as your best friend, and as your best friend, it is my duty and obligation to tell you when you're actin' like a nut. And I'm here to tell you, you're actin' like a nut."

"Why?" Carole-Anne said desperately. "Why is it so nutty that I love him? He's all I've ever wanted, and for once, I think I deserve to be happy."

"Listen to yourself, honey. All I'm hearin' is I, I, I, you, you, you. Have you learned nothing these last couple of years of walkin' in the Holy Ghost? When you and I converted to Pentecost, we knew nothing about this life. We knew nothing of the Holy Ghost, and we certainly knew nothing of the love of Christ. Carole-Anne, love is self-less. It's giving yourself, everything that you have, everything that you are, and going in faith that someone will do the same for you. And yes, you're willin', but, darlin', he isn't. He has his life, so let him live it. Without you."

Carole-Anne sat furious and broken, but in her heart, she knew Molly was right. But she would not stop fighting.

"No," Carole-Anne said plainly. "I won't let him go. Aren't you the one who always told me that if there was something that I wanted bad enough that I should fight for it?"

"No, actually I think it was that homeless man that one time. Remember, he had the sign?" Molly teased.

"Whatever," Carole-Anne said and rose from her seat. "I'm taking that advice. I refuse to be alone anymore, Moll. For once, I'm going to get what I want."

Carole-Anne left the restaurant determined she would get what she always wanted. And she would get it right now.

"Yeah, I guess I'll just pay for the meal since you invited me, cheater!" Molly yelled.

Carole-Anne smiled and waved. She was a woman on a mission. This was not a time for mindless chitchats and paying for half-eaten meals. She entered her green Pontiac, took out her cell phone, and dialed the number under Derek Cell.

"Derek, hi. It's Carole-Anne. Listen, we have to talk. Can you meet me in the church parking lot?"

# *Life*

"I said unto the Lord, Thou art my God; hear the voice of my supplication, O Lord. O God the Lord, the strength of my salvation, thou hast covered my head in the day of battle" (Ps. 140:7).

Paul's eyes watered when he heard his pastor read the scripture from Psalms. How God protected him and his family.

*What about Michelle? Did God protect her? No.*

*You see? God doesn't care about you. He laughs at your pain. He can't help you. Go back to the bottle.*

*No!*

*But it's the only thing that made you feel better. It gave you peace.*

*But my family—*

*They'll be fine.*

*No, they won't. They need me.*

Paul didn't know where these dark thoughts were coming from, but he knew certainly that they were not of God. He had given up drinking, made peace with his family, but there was something wanting him to go back to the life of despair.

"Church, if you need strength today, if you need your head covered for the battle, come. Come and receive redemption, protection, and strength."

This was Paul's first Sunday back to church since the death of his daughter. He didn't realize how much he missed his church and the love that radiated from the walls. Paul made up his mind that when altar call was made, he would not go up for prayer. He wasn't sure exactly why he had made that decision, but it felt right at the time. But now, he felt the tug of the Holy Ghost, and no was just not an option. Paul arose and began walking down the aisle.

*Turn back, now! They can't help you! God hates you!*

Paul quickened his steps, and once reaching the altar, he fell to his knees. With sobs, he cried, "Cover me, oh God. Protect me. Help me, Jesus!"

Touched by his anguish, the pastor called the elders of the church to pray with their fallen brother. Some prayed quietly for peace; others loudly rebuked the spirits that were attached to him.

Behind the crowd of men, stood Katie holding her two boys, weeping and praying. The ladies of the congregation stood behind her, praying along. Some wailed. Some wept, and some stood silently with their minds on the Lord.

"He's returning to you, Lord. My God, hold him. Hold him like you've held me." Katie's weeping turned to sobs of joy. Her family was being healed before her eyes. Her husband was in God's hands. He was safe, completely covered.

Paul stood, finally wiping his tears. A smile spread from across his face. He was at peace. He looked passed the crowd of men and saw his wife and children. They had been so strong. Katie had been so strong and brave to lose Michelle and then to lose her husband to alcohol, losing Michael because of his silence, and David who was forced to grow up so quickly. Katie stood her ground and continued to be obedient to the will of Jesus Christ. And now their family was being restored. He had seen his wife with new eyes. He respected and loved her more deeply than ever before.

David watched his father walk toward him, and he knew his real father had returned. He had kept his distance from his father since the day he hit him, but now, the man who made him feel confident and safe was back. And the old, abusive, angry father was gone forever.

Paul knelt down to look at his boys face-to-face. Michael stood confused, but David stood tall with tears running down his face and a smile on his lips.

"I love you," he said, looking at Michael and then at David. "I promise I will never do anything to hurt either of you ever again. I love you both so much." Paul sighed. "Will you forgive me for not being there for you?"

Michael, understanding, hugged his father and kissed his cheek. David stood, weeping.

"I love you, Dad," he said with a sob and hugged his father.

Paul laughed and rubbed his head. "I love you, son."

Paul rose from the ground and looked at his wife who was still weeping.

"I love you," Paul said, looking in to her eyes.

Katie sobbed, which was followed by laughter. "I love you too."

Paul opened his arms, and Katie walked in. A perfect fit. He lifted her chin to meet his gaze and took her hands in his and kissed them tenderly.

Though Katie and Paul only noticed each other, their Pentecostal congregation celebrated the family with whoops and hollers of praises to an almighty God. Katie knew this was a sign that her family was being restored.

*There's more.* Katie heard in the back of her mind

*More?* she thought.

*There's more to come.*

*Lord you've given us so much already.*

*Prepare yourself.*

*Lord, is this going to be a blessing or more trials? Our family has been through so much, Lord.*

*Be still.*

Katie dropped her thoughts, *I'm sorry. Let your will be done, Lord. I'll trust in you.*

Paul noticed Katie's troubled expression and gave her a questioning look.

Katie smiled. "I'll talk to you about it later."

Paul kissed his wife's forehead and turned his attention to the atmosphere of the altar call, which had made a dramatic change from restoration to praise and worship.

"Daddy?" Paul felt a tug on his suit jacket and looked to see Michael looking up at him.

"I'm hungry." Katie, Paul, and David stood, stunned, while Michael stood with his head up and smiling. "I really am hungry."

Paul lifted Michael and took him and his family in a joyful embrace.

# Fairy Tale

The night air was cool and brisk. Leila took previous precautions and wore her favorite light-blue jogging suit. She tied her hair in a loose ponytail and wore a blue headband around her head and large sunglasses to hide her eyes. No matter where she was, she looked like a jogger.

Boss had instructed her to wait until four in the morning so there would be no one in the streets to see her when she got rid of the body and ordered her not to wake him.

Leila did as she was told and waited until four in the morning to leave. She felt so close to freedom and fought the urge to bolt like lightning. But she knew if she went in to a full-blast run, she would be cause for suspicion. She felt it would be suspicious enough wearing sunglasses at night.

Leila jogged down the street then crossed and ran the opposite direction until she was right in front of the apartment complex and checked her watch. Once she heard police sirens, she crouched down by a parked car and slid underneath to have a clear view.

The police cars parked in front of the apartment complex and watched as the uniformed men, fully armed and alert exited the cars. Some stayed behind while a small group went into the apartment complex. Leila's heart pounded. Soon, she would see Boss, also known as Christopher Jenkins, in handcuffs and taken away to jail.

Since Boss instructed her to take the body after he had fallen asleep, she decided to use that time to escape. She rose and got dressed, making no sound. She took money from Boss's wallet and the secret stash he thought she didn't know about, stuffing as much cash in her purse as possible she left the room.

After, she decided to inspect the body bag. She slowly and quietly unzipped the bag and held in a gag as she saw the pale bruised body of Alicia Simms, one of Boss's prostitutes. Leila quickly zipped up the bag and dialed 911. Leila did not reveal her identity but told them enough to get their attention.

And now she watched eagerly, anxious to see her employer cuffed and taken away. But what she hadn't expected happened instead. Minutes later, the policemen came out of the building shaking their heads. They came down without Boss.

"What?" Leila whispered and climbed from under the car and watched in amazement as the cops entered their cars and drove away.

"I don't get it." She sighed.

"You should know better than try something so stupid, Leila." Leila gasped and turned to see Boss behind her holding a black pistol. "I'm not as stupid as you think." Leila shuddered at his icy tone.

Leila paced her breathing and, like a flash, was up and running, yet again, she wasn't quick enough. Boss lifted her from her sides and dropped her down hard. She had always underestimated Boss's strength and speed. Leila gasped from the pain and tried to scramble away, but Boss held her tight, beating her from the stomach up. Leila didn't even have the breath to scream or cry out in pain. Boss pulled her by the neck, tightening his grip on her throat. Leila clawed, kicked, and tried to scream, but Boss only held tighter. His eyes burned with murder. Leila stopped fighting, knowing she would end up just like Alicia, dumped in a Dumpster with no one to miss her.

Boss lifted his free hand and balled into a fist and swung hard into Leila's face. Once she went limp, Boss dropped her. Leila lay on the floor completely helpless as the world darkened around her.

# *Love*

Carole-Anne sat in her green Pontiac, waiting for Derek to show up. For once, she was going to fight for what she wanted and wasn't going to stop until she got it. Derek pulled up in his SUV, and Carole-Anne swallowed down her fear. It was now or never. Derek pulled up next to Carole-Anne and once again regretted coming to see her alone. He didn't know what to think about this woman. But he did know that he had to tread carefully and that he loved his fiancée. He reminded himself of this as he climbed out of his vehicle and walked toward her.

Both were outside of the cars. Carole-Anne realized that she had no clue what she was going to say to him. Derek looked at her and then quickly looked down to his feet. There was no denying it. There was something special about this driven woman who caught his attention. But he loved his fiancée. He loved his fiancée.

"You wanted to talk?" Derek said, hoping to skip the small talk.

She stood, studying him. He kept his hands in his pockets, and his eyes never met hers. But there was no turning back now. Taking a deep breath, Carole-Anne began, "I love you. And I think it's time you know the truth. I'm in love with you. All that you are, all that you do, I love. Your spirit and your passion for Christ touch the deepest part of my soul. In your eyes, I can see all your dreams come to life, dream and goals that I want to be a part of. And I know if you just give me a chance, us a chance, and I promise you, you won't regret it. I will love you like no one else will. I already do."

Carole-Anne didn't intend on shedding any tears, but they came. She said what she had to say, and now all she could do was to wait for the response.

Derek sighed. He didn't know what to say or how to feel. He knew Carole-Anne was speaking from her heart. But he also knew that the heart was a deceiver. He knew this. He loved his fiancée; he did not love Carole-Anne.

"Carole-Anne," Derek said with a sigh, "I'm engaged to a wonderful, godly woman, and I love her. I know in my spirit she is the only one for me."

Carole-Anne's tears fell, and her face dropped. It tore Derek apart to see her like this. But he knew that if he did not set things straight now, it would jeopardize everything he knew and loved.

Derek took Carole-Anne's hands and looked in her tear-filled eyes. "You are a beautiful woman with a beautiful and intense passion. One day, you will find a man, and he will love you the way you deserve to be loved. But I can't be that man."

"Yes, you could"—she sniffed—"we could be together. We could be happy."

Derek let go of her hands. "No, we wouldn't. I wouldn't be happy. And to be completely honest, are you really in love with me or just the idea of me?"

Carole-Anne could not answer. She could only follow her heart, and her heart was lonely and in love with a man she could not have.

Derek studied Carole-Anne and was touched by her tears. He wanted to hold her and comfort her, but he dared not touch her. Holding her hands, feeling them tremble in his, was enough to make his heart sink. He couldn't bring himself to touch her again.

"After the wedding, my wife and I will be leaving to northern California. I've been offered the position as youth pastor, and after a lot of praying and fasting, I've decided to take it. It'll be easier once I'm gone. You'll see." Derek turned and walked away, leaving Carole-Anne broken and shattered. The pain she felt was enough to make her feel lightheaded. But what else could be said? The man she loved did not love her, and now he was leaving forever.

She watched him drive away. The further he got from her sight, the more broken she became until finally, he was out her sight completely. She blinked away her tears and rubbed her eyes. Driven by anger and bitterness, she took out her cell from her purse. She refused to spend the night alone. If she couldn't be loved emotionally, then she would be loved physically by anyone who was willing to give it. She got rid of all of her old contacts that she knew when she lived in the world, but there was one number her mind would not let her forget—the number of Christopher "Boss" Jenkins.

# *Life*

Paul dreamed. He dreamed of Michelle, her long curly brown hair, light-brown eyes, and a smile that warmed the coldest of hearts. There she was, twirling and spinning like she so often did. And just like that, she was gone.

"Michelle!" Paul awoke, startled by the sound of his own voice.

"Daddy?" called the voice

"Michelle?" he called through the darkness of his room.

"No, Daddy, it's Michael." Michael came closer to his father.

"Oh. Michael," Paul said gruffly, still half-asleep. Paul reached over to his son and put his hand on his shoulder and squeezed lightly. "How are you, baby," Paul asked, rubbing his face.

"Good. I dream about her too Dad," Michael said, climbing up on his lap.

"You do? What do you dream about?"

"Sometimes, they're dreams that make me happy. I dream that she's home and we're playing just like we used to. But sometimes, they're sad. Sometimes I see her, and she looks at me and just walks away." Michael leaned against his father's chest and sighed.

"Will I ever see her again, Dad?"

Paul kissed Michael's forehead, and rubbing his head, he said, "You sure will. She'll be beautiful."

"My heart still hurts, Dad, when I think about her. Is that wrong?"

Paul swallowed down the lump that formed in his throat. "No, it's not wrong. She was a part of you, Michael. And she always will be as long as you keep her in your heart."

Michael sighed and wrapped his little arms around his father's neck.

"Mommy says it's time for dinner."

"All right, son, I'll be down soon."

Michael ran back downstairs and took his place amongst his toys and lost himself. Unknowing to Paul or Michael, there was a third party to their little conversation. Sitting on the other side of the wall with his ear pressed against it, David listened, feeling angry. Michelle never visited him in his sleep. Why didn't he ever dream about her? Hearing that the conversation was coming to a close, David ran downstairs and into the kitchen where his mother was preparing a delicious meal.

"Smells good, Mom."

Katie smiled and saw where David's eyes were averted. "I see you eyeing that cobbler."

David smiled. He wanted to take a closer look but knew if he got any closer to that juicy cobbler, he'd take a big bite and get a beating for it. *It might have been worth it,* he thought.

"It smells so good. Is it peach?"

"Mmmm. Your favorite." Katie walked over to her son and put her hand around his shoulders. "When it comes time for dessert, you'll get the first piece."

"Really? Awesome!"

"But only if you eat everything on your plate. I want it spotless, you hear me?"

"Yes, Mom," David said with a groan. He then walked over to the kitchen table and sat in one of the chairs, moving his leg up and down.

Katie saw the look on his face and knew something was bothering him.

"David?" she said while stirring gravy. "Will you help me set the table?"

"Sure."

She knew whatever was on David's mind would be easier if he were doing something constructive. David rose, grabbed the stepping stool, removed plates from the cabinets, and brought them to the table, and then he brought out knives, forks, and glasses. While doing so, his mind turned and struggled to comprehend.

"Are you going to tell me what's going on or frown at those plates all night?" Katie asked, watching him, studying him. He had grown so much since Michelle passed away. He had taken the role as father figure to Michael when Paul was overcome with grief, and many nights, Katie cried on David's shoulder. But he never cried on hers. He'd grown so much, too much. Sorrow for her children lingered in the air that she breathed.

*My babies. My poor babies,* she thought.

It seemed too much responsibility for an eleven-year-old to face. And now that he faced it, he grew up. He was a man stuck in an eleven-year-old's body. He was still a boy. Could her boy be reached?

*Lord, please let it be so!* she prayed.

David sat on one of the chairs and sighed, clutching a plate to his chest. Katie saw this and smiled sympathetically as she understood. Four plates were needed to set the table; David took out five. Katie took a break from her gravy and sat next to her son, whose tears fell to the floor.

"Mom," he began, "do you ever dream about Michelle?"

"Sure, I dream about her. All the time." David's shoulders dropped at the response.

"Why do you ask?"'

"I heard Michael and Dad talking upstairs. Dad was having a dream about Michelle, and Michael told him that sometimes, Michelle comes to visit him in his dreams and that they play together. Well, how come she never visits me?"

Katie shook her head. "It's not really Michelle that visits them, sweetie. It's just the memory of her. They're just dreams, and dreams aren't always what they seem."

"I miss her," David said shakily.

Katie put her hand to his cheek. "I know, I miss her too."

David continued to clutch the plate and sob. "Sometimes, I was so mean. Do you think she knew?" David asked with pleading eyes.

"Knew what?"

"That I loved her?"

"Oh sweetie." Katie reached over to her son, but he drew away.

"Sometimes I was so jealous of her. She and Michael were always playing, and I felt left out. Dad was always giving her everything and doing things with her. Sometimes, I felt so alone, like everybody just wanted Michelle. And sometimes, I wished that Michelle would just go away so that Michael and Dad could love me as much as they loved her." David shut his eyes and sobbed. "I never wanted her to die, Momma. I didn't mean for her to die!"

This time, Katie drew her son close before he could object. She held him tight, rocking him as she caressed his head. She wanted to shush him, but she knew all this time he was holding that in, so she would let him be. If he screamed, it would be fine with her.

"Baby, it wasn't your fault. These things, they happen. Michelle knew that you loved her. She knew she could always count on her big brother."

"Why did it have to happen? Why did Michelle have to die? You always taught me that God loves us and protects us, why didn't he protect Michelle? Why?! Why would he let Daddy hurt me that day?"

These questions tore at Katie's heart. Her son wanted answers but she had none. Katie prayed for words. She knew this was hard for them. Everyone else was able to deal with Michelle's death. Michael by his silence, Paul by his drinking, and Katie through Christ. But David never dealt with it. He never mourned, and though her family still mourned her passing, they were able to see the light at the end of the tunnel; they saw that life was meant to be lived for those who no longer lived. But David remained in the dark.

"The Lord sometimes allows things to happen to see where our faith is. He may have allowed Michelle to die because he needed us to be stronger. We're not the first family to lose someone, and maybe God is going to send someone to our church that has lost someone dear, and we'll be able to help them because we know what it feels like. And we're okay. Daddy's getting better, and Michael's getting better. God is still with us helping us."

David sniffed and shifted in his seat. "I guess, but did she really have to die?"

Katie couldn't answer him. She had asked that question so many times and received no answer. The only thing that ever came was scripture. "The Lord giveth and the Lord taketh away." The realization hurt her, but all she knew how to do was to let God have his way. "I can't answer your question. Some things we're just not meant to know. But we are meant to trust in God. If we trust Him, then He will take care of us. Michelle is with Jesus, and if we live the way Jesus wants us to live, then we'll see her again. Like it or not, Michelle is where she needs to be."

David placed the extra plate on the table and wiped his face. Though Michelle wasn't there anymore, he would always hold a special place for her in his heart, and there, her memory would live on for as long as he lived. Katie hugged her son and sighed. Yes, he had grown too much, but he was reachable. *Thank you Jesus!*

"Well, I'm starved. How about you?" Katie asked with a smile.

David looked up and gleamed, "I'm ready for that cobbler!" He laughed.

Katie chuckled. "Well, not before dinner." Katie hugged her son again and kissed him on the head.

"I love you, David," she said, squeezing him tight.

"I love you too, Mom. I can't breathe!" Katie squeezed tighter.

"Mom. Mom. Everything's going dark. Michelle, I'm coming!" Katie burst in to laughter as she let go of her son.

"Well, I'm glad to see you still have your sense of humor."

David arose and began to set the table again. he placed Michelle's plate back in the cupboard and, with that, said his last good-bye to his little sister.

"Hey, Mom." David turned with a smile on his face.

"Yes, sweetie," Katie said, returning to her gravy.

"Since Michelle isn't here anymore, can I have her piece of cobbler?"

Katie gasped and waved her utensil at him. "You keep playing like that, you won't get any peach cobbler! Now go finish setting the table!"

David hunched down and did as his mother told. Katie shook her head and held in her laughter.

# *Fairy Tale*

Everything was so bright. What was this place? Leila walked, unsure of her surroundings. She was in some kind of room with white walls and floors and lights. Oh, these lights were so bright. All she saw was blinding white.

Leila looked down and gasped at her appearance. She was covered in dirt. The more she wiped the dirt away, the more appeared. Clumps of mud and black ooze clung to her body becoming heavier and heavier. Leila worked frantically to get the mud and black stuff off of her. She didn't know what it was or where it came from; she just knew that she wanted it off. The mud surrounded her face and rolled down in heaps from her body. She did everything she could to wipe away the mess.

Leila closed her mouth tightly to prevent it from going in her mouth, down to her throat, and in to her heart. Leila fell to her hands and knees, exhausted from wiping and fear. She couldn't think of anything else to do.

She dared not open her mouth, but with everything in her, she cried out for help.

*Somebody help me, please!*

She watched as mud gathered at her hands and feet then dried and became like stone. She couldn't move. The mud dried over her body, keeping her trapped. Suddenly, the mud and oil began to disappear from her face. She breathed in deep and long then took in quick heaving breathes. She didn't realize in all the fear that the mud had begun to suffocate her. Leila coughed and groaned. Her lungs burned, and her heart was beating hard in her chest.

"Be still, daughter." Leila gasped and looked up to see no one around. Leila pulled and tugged, hoping she could break the stone, but it was no use.

"Be still."

"Who's there? Please, is anyone there? I need help. I...I can't. I'm trapped." Leila tried to blink away the tears, but they came and, one by one, hit the floor. Her desperation turned to anger, and her anger to panic.

"Please, help me!" she screamed. When no one answered, she gave way to despair and sobbed.

Suddenly, she felt a gentle hand upon her head. Slowly, she lifted her head and saw feet. Leila trembled as she realized a man was with her. She had never known a man to have perfect feet. But this person's feet were beautiful. She couldn't quite place what was so beautiful about his feet. On both feet was a tremendous scar that for some reason seeing it gave her chills. She knew these feet carried strength and power. The man that these feet belonged to no doubt carried a great and terrible burden.

Even his sandals seemed perfect, though they were worn and apparently incredibly old. She would even go so far as to say his sandals were ancient—ancient sandals that have seen ancient days.

Leila lifted her head higher and noticed his garment that came down to his ankles. His garment was white, whiter than their surroundings. She saw his hands; they too were perfect, just like his feet, though they were awfully scarred. She dared not look at his face, but it's not like she could. His face seemed to beam with light as bright as the sun. It was too bright to gaze upon.

"Who are you?" Leila whispered, suddenly filled with shame that this man is seeing her like this—filthy and trapped. His hand still rested on her head. Didn't he know she was dirty? How could he touch her when he was so clean?

"I have many names," he began. "But there is only one name under heaven and Earth that I will be called. I am Jesus."

Leila shook her head in disbelief. It couldn't be the same Jesus her mother told her about as a child. It was just a story, a fairy tale to make her feel safe. Safe. She hadn't felt safe in so long.

"You are safe with me, daughter. Stay with me. I will keep you safe." The scarred hands tenderly cupped Leila's face.

"Though you are unclean, I will make you white as snow."

Leila suddenly felt the weight of the dirt disappear.

"Though you are bound, I will make you free." The stone on Leila's hands and feet began to crumble, and she was free from their grasp. Leila stood in amazement. Her clothes weren't stained, and she was completely clean and was wearing garments that were white like snow. Leila laughed and twirled. For the first time in her life, she felt completely alive and free. Remembering the man who stood before her, she stopped and looked at him. His face still shone brightly causing her to squint.

"Take my hand," He said and held out his scarred hands and waited for Leila to take hold. Leila felt overwhelmed by his hands that were scarred but powerful. What she felt was neither fear nor doubt. She was overwhelmed with love. Love so passionate it brought tears to her eyes. It reached passed her heart and into the very depths of her soul. Leila held his hands and felt soothing warmth that cascaded throughout her entire body.

"Don't let go of me, Leila, for I will never let go of you."

Leila felt the ground tremble beneath her, and a strong wind blew about them. She watched as the light from His face grew painfully brighter and brighter until it covered the entire room.

Leila awoke with the sun shining in her face. Then suddenly darkened by the tall dark figure who stood over her.

"Bet you'll think twice before you do somethin' like that again, huh, Lil'Mama?"

Leila groaned and once again fell in to darkness.

# *Love*

Christopher Jenkins had tall, dark, and handsome written all over him. It was no wonder why Carole-Anne had fallen for him once upon a time. Though they were lovers in the past, Carole-Anne made it a point to never get too attached to him. They were lovers, and that was it.

She knew Chris was a man who could smooth-talk his way out of any situation. She knew he had a weak spot for the ladies, especially the younger ones. She also knew he was a liar, a thief, and a murderer. He was a mastermind. If you saw a knife that was dripping with blood, he would convince you it was a simple butter knife and the blood was actually honey.

She knew who and what Chris was. He was a drug dealer, most if not all the drugs she received from the past were from him. And he was a pimp. He sold women for pleasure; the majority of his money came from the women he sold.

Surprisingly, he had never once offered her a job in his business. He would hint to her once or twice that it was good money, but he never pressured her.

She knew this was an awful idea. Everything inside her screamed to turn back, but ignoring her conscience, she moved on. She was determined to be loved tonight, even if it was with a man who held no love for her in his heart. She walked the familiar hall and was soon standing in front of Chris's apartment door. What if Chris didn't recognize her? It had been years since she'd seen him. She had not yet known of the truth of Pentecost when she knew Chris. Her hair was short and dyed blonde. Now that she was saved, baptized in

Jesus's name and filled with the Holy Ghost, her appearance began to gradually change. The more she studied her Bible, she learned that a woman's hair was considered to be her glory and even the woman's power and was considered a shame to her and God if she cut it. She hadn't brought scissors to her hair since. Her hair had grown and reached the small of her back and was now her natural hair color of brown.

When she knew Chris, she dressed in short skirts or shorts and a form-fitting tank top. Now she was dressed modestly with an off-white, high-necked blouse with quarter-length sleeves and long red skirt and sash. She was almost certain that Chris would not recognize her. She began to hope that he wouldn't. Forcefully, Carole-Anne knocked on the door before she changed her mind and soon heard the familiar voice on the other side of the door.

"Who is it?" the voice yelled, sounding tough.

Carole-Anne suddenly lost her voice and forced it out, "It's Carole-Anne!"

Carole-Anne sighed as she heard the door unlock and saw the door opened slightly, just enough so that Chris could inspect the scene first. He had always been paranoid. The door suddenly swung open, and Chris stood and laughed, shining his silver grill.

Before Carole-Anne could say another word, Chris picked her up and swung her around. Carole-Anne laughed.

"Oh girl! I've missed you! Wait, wait." Chris set her down and placed his hand over his mouth and inspected the lady that stood in front of him.

"You look different. Your hair is so long! You look gorgeous, girl!"

"Oh yeah, I guess I have changed a bit since you last saw me." Carole-Anne blushed.

"A bit? Nah, girl, you've changed a lot. You look grown, like a real woman. Look at you, no makeup, long hair, skirt. If I didn't know any better, I'd say you were a churchgoer. Sanctified and filled with the Holy Ghost as my grandma used to say."

Carole-Anne chuckled nervously. She had to change the subject.

"So what about you? You've changed too. I see you got a grill." Chris smiled, showing his glistening silver teeth.

"Yeah, had to bling it up a bit."

"Mmmm." Carole-Anne looked around the apartment. It had changed much since she last saw it. It was clean and given a completely new look. The walls were white, which made the apartment look bigger and more expensive. The floors were wooden and shined. His couch and chairs were black leather, forty-two-inch plasma screen TV, and an entertainment center that held the TV, CDs, and countless DVDs.

"This is some place. You've gotten a whole bunch of new toys the last couple of years."

"That's the joy of money, Ma." Carole-Anne smiled. "So you still tight with yo girl?" he asked, walking to his fridge and taking out a beer.

"Who, Molly?"

"Yeah, her. How she doin'?"

"She's great. She's married now."

Chris choked on his beer.

"Molly?"

"Yeah, she got married a little over a year ago."

"Wow, never thought she'd get hitched."

Carole-Anne smiled. Chris watched her intently. She had changed so much. She had something that she never had before—confidence and grace. Chris walked over to her and put his hand gently on the back of her neck and brought her to him in a slow, careful kiss.

"I've missed you." He sighed. She wrapped her arms around him, relieved that someone had missed her. At least someone wanted her.

"Man, girl, you would make me some mad money." Carole-Anne's eyes widened, and her face heated. "Nah," Chris laughed, "I've always wanted you to myself. And now I've got you." He helped himself to the back of her neck.

"Um, Chris...I don't think this is such a good idea."

Chris removed himself from her neck and smiled. "You gonna try and toy with me now, Lil' Mama?" Chris circled her. He was like a vulture waiting for his prey to die. Carole-Anne knew being with him would cause her to die spiritually, and once she was dead, Chris could do what he wanted with what remained of her.

Lingering behind Carole-Anne, Chris rubbed her neck and whispered words that enticed her senses. Her heart pounded, not with lust but with fear. She felt as though she were on the edge of a cliff, just inches away from certain death.

"Chris, this was a mistake." She breathed. "I shouldn't have come."

"Well, you're here, Ma. Might as well make the best of it." He kissed her neck again and took her hand to lead her.

"Chris, I can't. This was a mistake." She took her hand away from his grasp.

"What, are you serious?"

"I shouldn't have come."

"So what, you just came to toy with me or what?"

"No—"

"I mean you call me up and show up out of nowhere. You came to see me, Lil' Mama, and now you just wanna run out? You know more than anyone not to run out on me. Who do you think I am?"

"Chris, I...I'm just going to go."

"Nah, Lil' Mama, here's what imma do. I'm gonna go into my room. You sit out here, and you think about it." Chris walked to Carole-Anne and kissed her. She melted under his touch and knew he had her. He smiled, shining his grill.

"Don't make me wait too long, or I'll come get you myself." Chris walked to his bedroom and shut the door behind him. Carole-Anne sighed, relieved that Chris had given her the option to stay or go. Chris was dangerous and could have easily taken advantage of her. But for some reason, Chris had treated her differently than any other woman who came across his path; that to her was an act of God. But what of love? She had come here because she longed to be loved in any way, shape, or form. But now, her conscience and years of following after God and His law stopped her.

*Go ahead and go to him. You're lonely. He can keep you company tonight. Then afterward you can repent. You deserve to be loved, don't you?*

Carole-Anne couldn't move or think. All she knew was that love was just a few feet away from her. Here was someone waiting to love her. He was waiting for *her.* Carole-Anne sighed. Every so often, she thought she heard a noise that sounded like a groan, and she felt shame as she thought of it as her spirit groaning. She thought of Jesus at the tomb of Lazarus. All among him were people mourning over the death of Lazarus, and in despair, Jesus groaned. Could He be groaning now because of her behavior? She continued to hear the groaning as she wrestled with her mind and body. She walked to Chris's door and put her hand on the doorknob and pushed away her guilt and shame as she began to enter the bedroom.

# *Life*

Katie sat at her kitchen table looking at old family pictures and sighing heavily. She flipped through the pages of her life and reminisced in her mind. It was early; the boys and Paul were still asleep, and she enjoyed her coffee and scrapbook. Soon Paul entered the kitchen and grabbed himself a cup of coffee and sat next to his wife.

"What are you doing?" he said, rubbing her hand.

Katie sighed. "I'm looking at pictures."

Paul leaned over to see the picture that caught Katie's attention. Two girls—who resembled each other greatly, almost twin like—hugging each other and smiling, but it was evident that one was older than the other.

"Is it her birthday today?"

Katie nodded. Paul rubbed her back and kissed her forehead.

"You'd think after all these years I would have forgotten her by now."

Paul shook his head. "She was your sister. You both were so close."

"But that didn't stop her, did it?" Katie said, flipping pages.

"Katie, you have to let that go and forgive her. If not, you'll always have that bitterness."

"She left, Paul. She left me alone," Katie said through tears.

"I know, baby."

"No, you don't know. She was my best friend."

Paul always felt uncomfortable talking about the things that happened to Katie in the past, but he knew she had to let it out, or it would eat her alive.

"Tell me what happened, Katie."

"She was so happy with him. I've never seen her so happy before. But my mom and dad didn't like him. They sensed something in him. They saw behind his charm and his smile. They saw the darkness in him. But Grace was blinded by love for him. One night, I heard my parents and her fighting. Apparently, he proposed to her, and my parents didn't want her seeing him anymore. That night, she packed her things, and we never saw her again. My dad made phone call after phone call; my mother sat at the window, keeping watch. She hardly ever slept, and if she did, she slept at the window. They never found her, and we never heard from her again, and there was no record of her husband, Max Carter. After a while we accepted that she was dead. We refused to believe that she was alive and avoiding us. We were such a close family. So we just told ourselves that she died. And that was the end of my sister, Grace."

"Do you believe that she's dead?" Paul asked, rubbing her shoulders.

"I never believed it. Not once. I never spoke to my parents about it because it upset them, but I always believed that she was out there somewhere, alive. But now I do believe that she is dead."

"Why now?"

"One night, several years ago, I woke up in a cold sweat. I dreamed about Grace. She was crying and saying something over and over again. She was crying out to me. And then she was gone. I knew then that she died."

"Why haven't you told me?"

"I didn't find it important. Everyone already thought she was dead. What difference did it make if I knew in my heart that she was?"

"What was she saying over and over again?"

"Some name. Leila is what it sounded like."

"Leila? What do you think that means?"

"I don't know. I never put much thought about it."

"Leila," Paul said slowly and watched Katie close her photo album and began to prepare breakfast for her family.

# Fairy Tale

Leila awoke and groaned. Her entire body hurt. She could barely muster the strength to call for help. She looked at her surroundings and found that she was in Boss's guest bathroom. Her jumpsuit was covered with blood, and she couldn't see out of one eye. She tried to raise herself up, but the pain was unbearable. With a groan, she fell back down and slipped into unconsciousness.

# *Love*

Carole-Anne slowly opened the bedroom door and saw that Chris was in a deep sleep, and she had no intention of waking him.

Carole-Anne quietly and quickly left the room and slowly closed the bedroom door behind her. She leaned against the door and wept. God had saved her from making a terrible decision. Her heart was heavy with guilt. Though she hadn't committed the sinful act, she had brought herself just inches away from it. Through God's mercy, He had made a way out of it. Even now she felt shame. How could she be so desperate? How could she bring herself to beg for forgiveness? She hadn't changed at all from her old self. She was no different from the women Chris sold.

*Be still.*

*What? No, don't talk to me. I'm not worthy.*

*Be still.*

Carole-Anne bit her bottom lip to keep herself from sobbing. She had wanted to be loved. She wanted to lay down with that man. Even now, something inside her cried for physical love. How could he speak to her now? How could she be still now?

*Be still. Listen.*

She controlled her breathing and leaned silently against the door. She couldn't hear anything. She heard Chris snoring lightly; she heard the ticking of a nearby clock. But she heard nothing out of the ordinary. Nothing. Wait. She heard it, groaning. It was distant but coming from somewhere in the apartment. She listened as the groaning became louder.

Carole-Anne followed the sound of groans. She followed it into a small hallway and stopped at Chris's guest bathroom where the groans were the loudest. The door had not been completely closed and was open just a crack. She looked through the small opening and saw a young girl lying on the floor wearing a bright-blue jogging suit, which was stained with blood.

Carole-Anne gasped and pushed the door open and ran to the girl. She was trembling and in much pain. Her face was badly bruised and a gash on the side of her forehead.

"Oh." Carole-Anne touched her cheek and moved a strand of black hair from her face. She watched as the girl's eyes fluttered open.

"Don't be afraid," she whispered. I won't hurt you. Did Chris do this to you?"

The girl lightly nodded and whispered, "Boss."

"Boss? You work for him?" The girl nodded lightly. *She's so young! Eighteen at most!*

Carole-Anne lifted the young girl and braced herself for the extra weight. "What's your name?" Carole-Anne grunted.

"Leila," the girl whispered weakly.

"Such a pretty name. All right, Leila, I'm going to get you out of here. I'm going to get you some help. Now put your arm around my neck. That's it. Now hold on."

Leila did as she was told and allowed the lady to carry her. Carole-Anne was surprised at how light she was. From the feel of Leila's body, she guessed that she was malnourished. Leila groaned softly and fell into unconsciousness again. Carole-Anne tried to walk quickly, careful not to hurt Leila any further. The hallway was small but seemed to take forever to get out of. Carole-Anne picked up her pace and hummed a song to ease her anxiety. Once out of that tiny hallway, Carole-Anne breathed easier. She was half out. Just ten feet away was the door, and outside was her freedom. Carole-Anne looked around the apartment; everything was still and quiet. She gulped down her fear and walked out in to the open. She felt like a deer coming out from the protection of the trees into an open wide meadow with nowhere to hide. Her heart pounded against the silence, and sweat ran down her face.

Leila groaned and began to stir.

"You're hurting me." She groaned. With a gasp, she realized she was holding Leila very tight her fingers dug in to her body.

"I'm sorry," Carole-Anne whispered and released her tight grip. *What am I doing?* Carole-Anne asked herself. She had been standing still in the middle of the room with the door just five feet away. She rushed to the door and reached out her hand to grab the knob and froze in place when she heard a small click. The sound was all too familiar to her.

She remembered being threatened by her ex-husband. She remembered the feel of the cold weapon pressed to her head as he threatened to kill her if she didn't get an abortion. When she never answered him, he pressed the lever to let her know the gun was ready to fire. She would never forget that sound or the terror she felt because of it.

Carole-Anne turned around slowly, and there sitting on the couch was Chris who casually smoked a cigarette, all the while aiming the pistol at her.

"Ya know, I think everybody thinks I'm stupid. Alicia thought I was stupid, and what happened to Alicia? She got thrown out with the rest of the garbage. Leila thought I was stupid, and I beat the stupid right outta her. What about you, Annie? Do you think I'm stupid?"

Chris inhaled his cigarette and let out a puff of smoke then smiled at Carole-Anne. A smile that was full of cold malice. Chris arose and walked coolly toward the woman and the unconscious teenager. He looked at Carole-Anne and moved a strand of brown hair from her face and then looked down at Leila. Her face was black and blue. Her right eye was swollen shut, and her hair was dirty and oily.

"Beautiful, ain't she? She's worth the trouble, believe it or not. She makes me a lot of money. She's a favorite in the business. Not to mention I get to have her, free of charge." Chris laughed maliciously.

Carole-Anne said no words. She only prayed silently, *Lord, please see us out of this. Keep us, God. Protect us from the evil one. In Jesus name.*

Chris looked at Carole-Anne and held out his hands.

"Give her to me, Anne," he said with a smile on his face. She shook her head. "Give her to me, and you can go home. No one gets hurt. Just give her to me."

"No Chris. She's hurt bad. She needs a doctor."

"How long have you known me, Ma? No doubt you've known me long enough to know not to get in my way." He lifted the gun to her face. "So what's it gonna be?" Chris touched the gun to Carole-Anne's temple. She felt her blood tremble, but surprisingly, her outside did not.

"I'm not leaving her, Chris."

Chris sighed, and a touch of sadness crossed his face. "Wrong choice. Good-bye, Anne."

Carol-Anne closed her eyes and whispered the name of Jesus, for the last sound she heard was the explosion of a gun.

# Life

"Life doesn't always turn out like we want it to. Sometimes we find that in life, when things go wrong, our weaknesses take over." Paul looked out into the congregation. Some seemed to hang on his every word while others wept silently in their pews.

"As many of you know, my daughter, Michelle, was run over and killed several months ago. Michelle was the kind of child that brought light to any room. Like the rest of my children, she added something very special to my family. She brought us together. When we were all in different areas of the house, doing our own thing, she would drag everyone outside to play together as a family. She was Daddy's little girl. When we lost her, I lost sight of everything else in my life—my wife, my boys, nothing seemed important. Nothing except alcohol." As Paul continued with his testimony of his victory over grief and alcoholism, Katie watched with a smile on her lips and tears in her eyes.

He stood so tall now. Of course, he still grieved over Michelle's passing as she did. But now, they grieved together. They were a comfort to each other. Katie smiled and thanked God that He brought them through those hardships.

"Through all of this," Paul continued, "I've learned to trust in God. I don't know why He chose my family to carry this burden or why he took Michelle, but I do know that God knows what He's doing, and though we walk away from Him, He will never walk away from us. May the Lord bless you."

The congregation stood and applauded as Paul made his way down the platform and back to his seat next to Katie. Paul took her hands and brought them to his lips. Her heart skipped a beat. She felt as though she were falling in love all over again. They sat together and listened to the next person who gave their testimony.

After the testimonial service was done, several members of the church came to shake Paul's hand and expressed their gratitude for sharing his testimony. One young man in particular came to shake his hand. His name was Matthew Graves, who was one of the young leaders for the congregation.

"Brother Paul!" Matthew smiled and greeted him with a firm handshake.

"Brother Matthew." Paul smiled and returned the greeting with a warm hug.

"That was an amazing testimony! It made my eyes leak a little bit, but *shhh*, don't pass that around."

Paul chuckled. "Your secret's safe with me. And your testimony! It was very brave of you."

Matthew sighed and looked to the ground. He still could not believe he had confessed his fornications to the entire congregation, who saw him as a promising young leader. It seemed too terrifying to fathom. He thought for sure stones would be tossed. Instead, he was shown grace and understanding. The world was such an enticing place especially for someone like him who was single. He had found a church, and now that he knew this was the place God wanted him, he was afraid. He knew if he began to study the Word of God, then he would know what to do and what not to do according to God's law. He was so new to this faith. He was just a baby trying to crawl. Confessing his struggles with the congregation made him hope that maybe someone could help him; maybe someone also had struggles with lusts of the flesh.

"It was hard. I still feel like I let everyone down."

"Well, I'm sure you'll feel a lot more of that the more you learn. But the Lord sees your heart. And you've repented. He forgives you, and we do too. Just don't take His love and mercy for granted because He is the God of judgment. And He will judge."

"I understand." Matthew smiled and shook his hand. Matthew held a high respect for Paul. Paul was maybe ten years older than

Matthew, give or take a year, but he knew he could come to Paul seeking advice.

"It was good to see you. I have to go meet with Pastor now. Pray for me," Matthew said with a laugh.

"I will. Everything will be fine." Paul watched as the young man made his way through the congregation and knew that one day, Matthew would be a great leader if he would just yield fully to the will of God.

Paul felt a light touch on his arm and turned to see his wife smiling up at him. Paul took her into his arms and held her, breathing her in. She fit him so perfectly, every day, he seemed to fall more in love with his wife. Katie sighed and took in the scent of her husband and was overjoyed that she would go home to him every day for the rest of her life. That thought filled her with an overwhelming sense of peace.

"Excuse me."

Paul and Katie broke their embrace and looked at the apologetic eyes of Carole-Anne Welsch, the youth's Sunday school teacher. Katie greeted her with a surprised smile.

"Carole-Anne!" Katie hugged her warmly. "How are you, I haven't seen you in weeks!"

"I know." Carole-Anne laughed. "Paul"—she held out her hand and Paul shook it warmly—"I heard your testimony rocked the house. Not a dry eye in the place from what I was told. I'm sorry I missed it."

Paul blushed. "Were you teaching Sunday school this morning?" Katie asked.

"No, I asked Molly to teach this morning. I just now made it to church."

"Oh." Katie looked at her and then at Paul in confusion.

"May I speak to you both, in private?" Carole-Anne asked.

Katie looked at her husband. "Of course," Paul said and led the two ladies outside of the church and into the parking lot.

"So," started Katie, "what's up?"

Carole-Anne looked at Katie and noticed the similarities. But she wouldn't know for sure unless she asked.

"Katie, I know we are not very close friends, but I do like to think of us as friends," Carole-Anne began.

"Well, of course, we are!" Katie laughed.

"Good. Because this question I'm about to ask you may seem a bit odd, but I need to know. Does the name Leila mean anything to you?"

Katie was shocked by the question. "Leila? Um..."

"Why do you ask?" Paul jumped in, seeing Katie's discomfort. Carole-Anne sighed and began to tell how she came to find a girl named Leila who strangely resembled Katie.

"She looks so much like Katie. I just had to find out if this girl could be related to you."

Katie stood. Her hand was cupped over heart. Her face was pale, and her eyes were wide with shock.

"Katie?" Paul said, touching her arm. "Are you all right?"

Katie took a deep breath and nodded.

"Her name is Leila?" Katie said, trying to focus on taking deep breaths.

"Yes," Carole-Anne answered. "Leila Carter." Katie shook her head in disbelief. Carole-Anne was puzzled by Katie's reaction, but she apparently had dug up something from Katie's past. "Katie, will you please tell me if you know this girl?"

"My sister," Katie began, "was in love with a man named Max Carter. My parents didn't approve of him. And when he proposed to her, they forbid her from ever seeing him again. So she ran away to be with him. That was the last time I ever seen or heard of my sister." Katie sighed and swallowed down her emotion. "One night, several years ago, I dreamt about my sister. She was crying and saying this name over and over and over again. Leila, Leila, Leila. And she looked at me and reached out and then disappeared. I knew then that she died."

"Oh." Carole-Anne looked at the ground. "You and your sister, you two look a lot alike?"

"Almost identical," Paul said, putting an arm around his wife. "Except, Katie has brown hair, and her sister had black hair."

"People thought we were twins," Katie said sadly.

"I-I'm sorry, Katie," Carole-Anne said, feeling terrible.

"So where's the girl?" Paul asked.

"She's in the hospital now. She's pretty banged up, but she'll be fine. The thing is, the police want to put her in to foster care, but she's eighteen now. She's no longer considered a minor, and it's harder for people to take in the older ones. But now that we know she has relatives—"

"Are you saying we should take in this kid we don't even know?" Paul asked.

Carole-Anne sighed. "I just wanted to tell you. She's not ready to leave the hospital yet. And I would like her to stay with me for a couple of days, and that'll give you time to think about it."

Katie wanted to say yes immediately, but the look on her husband's face told her to wait.

"We'll talk about it and call you when we've decided," Katie said, hugging her husband.

"Great. Good. Okay. Yeah." Carole-Anne laughed and left the couple to their thoughts.

# *Fairy Tale*

Once again, the dream came. The white surroundings, the filth that trapped her and the man that set her free.

"Don't let go of me, Leila," the man said, "for I will never let go of you."

The voice was so soft and yet so powerful. Surely, the voice belonged to a man with much authority.

Leila awoke with a sigh and smiled lightly at her warm and friendly environment. She was glad to finally be out of the hospital, out of that daily reminder of the mess she had let herself get into. She thought about ending her life so many times, but something inside her pulled to fight and to live.

And now Boss had been incarcerated for murder and attempted murder on two accounts. Though she no longer had to worry about Christopher Jenkins, also known as Boss, she did though, worry about where she would stay. She was no longer considered a minor, and without a job, she could not afford her own place. Whichever way she looked at it, the situation seemed hopeless. That is, until Carole-Anne showed up and gave her a place to stay. Carole-Anne opened her home to her, and Leila was able to rest easy knowing that she was safe with this woman.

Leila turned on her side and snuggled under the large plush blankets. She loved Carole-Anne's guest bedroom. The walls were a very soft brown and ascended with yellow and light blue. The room reminded her of a beach (not that she had ever been), but she would assume the beach would be warm and beautiful, a place where worries and fears didn't exist at least for a period of time. Leila smiled and promised herself that one day, she would take a trip to the beach and feel the warm sand beneath her feet and the warmth of the sun on her face.

"One day." Leila sighed.

Leila lazily rolled out of bed and stretched until several bones in her body cracked and popped, leaving her loose and relaxed. It had been two days since coming here from the hospital, and she felt more at home every day. Carole-Anne was wonderful, so understanding and kind. It was strange for Leila to see someone who was kind and sought nothing in return for her kindness. Leila left the room and was soon welcomed by the smell of bacon. Leila's mouth watered and ran to the bathroom and quickly brushed her teeth. She was apprehensive to Carole-Anne's kindness, but she knew one thing: the woman knew her way around the kitchen. Leila then walked briskly to the kitchen, and there she saw the most beautiful thing. If there was a heaven, it was on Carole-Anne's dining table. It was the most glorious thing she'd ever seen. The table was full of steaming breakfast foods: eggs, pancakes, sausage and bacon, cinnamon toast, biscuits and gravy, fruit and yogurt. She was sure at any minute she would cry. Leila looked toward the kitchen and saw Carole-Anne bent over with her head in her refrigerator, muttering to herself. Soon Carole-Anne emerged, holding a pitcher of orange juice and a gallon of milk.

"Oh, you're up!" Carole-Anne said happily.

"What do you prefer? Orange juice or milk?"

Leila smiled. "Orange juice would be great."

Carole-Anne smiled and put the milk back in the fridge.

"Carole-Anne, I can't believe you cooked all this. I could hug you!"

Carole-Anne laughed. "Well, go ahead and help yourself. There's plenty."

Leila turned to marvel at the spread, and for some strange reason, she began to feel melancholy.

Carole-Anne noticed her glum expression and walked to her. "What's wrong, Leila."

"Nothing. It's nothing. It's just, no one's ever been this nice to me before. And I can't help think there's some motive behind it. But I have no clue what that motive would be, except—"

"Except what?"

"That there really is no motive. And that you're doing all this out of love."

Leila tried to hold back the tears, but for once in her life, she felt no shame in letting them role down her cheek.

"It is with love."

"But you don't even know me."

"I don't have to. All I know is that God created you, and we are a part of His kingdom. We are His children, and He is our Father. So if He is my Father and He is your Father, then that makes us sisters."

"God does not exist. He is not my father. He's just a story. A sweet little bedtime story."

"The sweetest," Carole-Anne said smiling. "Go on and eat. It's going to be a very interesting day."

Paying no attention to her last comment, Leila sat at the table debating what to eat first. Never in her life had she ever seen so much food! Boss never allowed her to eat what she wanted. She would snack on nuts while Boss would eat pizza and burgers right in front of her. On occasion, she would eat a salad, and on rare occasions, Boss would allow some meat in her salad. He would allow her to eat it only to throw it back up again. But there would be none of that now; she would eat until her heart was content. Though she knew she would feel guilty about it later and force herself to throw up, but that was later, and later wasn't now. Now she had a table full of delicious food and was going to enjoy every bit of it.

Carole-Anne placed a plate in front of Leila and put down a glass and filled it with orange juice. "Dig in, chick!" Carole-Anne said, excited for the food as well.

"Do you cook like this all the time?" Leila asked with a mouthful of scrambled eggs.

"Oh no. Only on certain occasions, or when I'm stressed. But today was for a special occasion." Carole-Anne smiled.

"Man, if I were a dude, I'd totally propose to you, like, right now!" Leila laughed.

"I'm glad you like it. I enjoy having someone to cook for. Cooking for yourself gets tedious after a while."

Leila grabbed two more pancakes and poured a large helping of syrup on top.

"You don't have a man to cook for?" Leila asked with her mouth full.

"No." Carole-Anne said sadly, "It's been a very long time since I've cooked for someone other than myself."

"Don't you have friends come over?" Leila asked.

"Well, most of my friends are married with children. They have their own lives."

Leila didn't want to seem nosey, but she wanted to know about this woman and her past. "Haven't you ever been married?"

"I almost was, once. When I was very young."

Leila studied Carole-Anne. "What happened? Did you get cold feet?"

"Something like that. He was abusive and controlling and, at times, could be very cruel. I was about your age when we got engaged. At that time, the both of us were heavily involved in drugs, and then I found out that I was pregnant. When I told him we were going to have a baby, he became angry. He threatened to kill me if I didn't get rid of the baby."

"Where were you're parents?"

"They kicked me out when I was sixteen. I was a wild child, and they couldn't put up with me, so they kicked me out, and then I met Eddie."

"So what happened to the baby?"

"I got the abortion, and afterward, I fell into severe depression. I even tried to kill myself a couple of times. Sometimes, I got real close. Eventually, Eddie left me, and I had nowhere to go. I was homeless for a while, and one day, I was walking around town, and Chris or Boss drove by and offered me a place to stay. We became lovers after that. He helped me find a job at a nearby grocery store and taught me all I needed to know about making it on my own. We were still doing drugs, and one night, I woke up because of a pain in my stomach. When I got to the bathroom, there was blood everywhere."

"You were pregnant," Leila said wide-eyed.

"Yes, I had a miscarriage because of all the drugs. So after that, I quit doing drugs. But Chris did more and more, and then he got his business. I realized if I wanted to live a changed life, then I had to leave. So I walked away. By that time, I had enough money saved up to be on my own. So I called up my best friend, who had her own apartment and asked if I could move in. After that, things got better. Molly started to go to church, and she quit drinking. Once I saw the changes in her, I decided to go to church too. We were baptized together in Jesus's name. Sometime after that, Molly met Jim, got married, and I moved here with the hopes that I could fill this house with a family of my own. But it hasn't happened yet."

Leila poked at her eggs. "So, you're a Christian now?"

"Yes, I am."

"So what were you doing in Boss's house the day you found me?"

Carole-Anne sighed. She knew the question would come up sooner or later. "I was...it's hard to explain. I was heartbroken. I loved this man, and he didn't love me. He rejected me. I felt alone and unlovable. I just wanted to be loved by someone, and I knew Chris would be the only person willing to love me even if it was for one night. It was a mistake, but God saved me and led me to you." She smiled.

"God?" Leila rolled her eyes. "Boss said God was something people believed in because they couldn't handle the fact that life was nothing. God had nothing to do with you finding me that day. God does not exist. This Jesus guy doesn't exist either."

Carole-Anne remained silent.

"Ya know, my mom believed in that guy, Jesus. I remember her telling me that when I was afraid, all I had to do was to call His name, and He would protect me. She said He would always be with me. But He wasn't there for my mom. My mom's in the dirt now, probably dust by now. He wasn't with her, was He? Was He with me when my dad would sneak into my bedroom at night and rape me?

If He was, He wouldn't have let those things happen. If He was such a protector, then how come He didn't protect me and my mom?"

Carole-Anne looked at the angry eyes of the teenager. She had no words. "I don't know."

Leila continued eating, despite the knot that had formed in her stomach. If everything was just a lie, then what about the dreams?

"Leila?" Leila looked up at Carole-Anne whose face was stricken with sadness. Suddenly, the knot in her stomach got tighter. "There are some people coming over today. They've been anxious to meet you."

"Me?" Leila questioned

"Yes. It's in their best interest that they talk to you and that you talk to them."

"But I don't know them."

"You will. They're a married couple. The husband is named Paul, and the wife's name is Katie. They'll be able to answer a lot of your questions about your parents, and maybe you'll answer a couple of theirs too."

Leila rolled her eyes. "Whatever." She figured they were social workers. Whoever they were, she knew they would not be able to answer any of her questions.

# *Love*

One month had passed since Carole-Anne found Leila, and now Leila was in the custody of her aunt and uncle. She lived with Paul and Katie and was doing well. She refused to come to church, but she was a work in progress. With the Lord's help, she knew Leila would turn around. Yes, a month had passed, but Carole-Anne felt no different. She still felt lonely and unlovable, especially today. For today, Carole-Anne watched with sorrow as the beautiful bride made her way to the smiling groom, her groom. She still loved him with everything that was in her. But he did not love her, so she had no choice but to let him go and support him on what he considered the happiest day in his life.

The bride made her way down the aisle and was soon hand in hand with the love-struck groom. The congregation sat and listened as the minister led the ceremonies for the happy couple. Carole-Anne swallowed the lump that had formed in her throat and fought not to picture herself in the bride's place. She watched and smiled when the minister reminisced about their dating experience and applauded along when the groom ended the ceremony by giving the bride a long, tender kiss. Outside, she seemed just as content as everyone else, but inside, she was screaming. A hand lightly brushed Carole-Anne's shoulder, and before she could show her true feelings, she smiled in hopes to cover them.

"Are you okay?" Molly asked.

Carole-Anne sighed and continued to smile. "Not really. But I will be," she said, hopeful.

"Yeah, you will," Molly agreed. "You gonna go to the reception?"

Carole-Anne shook her head. "I don't think so. I think I'll just go and congratulate them and go on home."

Molly nodded. "That sounds good. Let's do it!"

Carole-Anne rolled her eyes to look at her friend. "Let's? As in let us? As in we?" Carole-Anne joked.

"Yeah, why not? We'll stay up late, watch chick flicks, and eat popcorn, dish on the hot guys, and talk about things we don't understand. You know a real girls night!"

Carole-Anne shook her head. "I don't think I'm up for that, Moll."

"Which is exactly why we should do it! Carole-Anne, come on, you're hurting. And what better way to take your mind off the pain than with a good old-fashioned sleepover?"

"What about Jim?"

"He'll be happy to have a break from me for a night. We're doing it! Whether you like it or not, we're doing it!"

Carole-Anne laughed and put an arm around her friend. She knew just what to do to pull her out of the slums.

"All right, let's do it."

"Yes! You'll see, Carole-Anne, I'll order pizza, pick up some ice-cream. It'll be great!"

"All right, I trust you."

Carole-Anne may have been brokenhearted, but at least God was merciful enough to find her a friend who would pick up the pieces.

"Hello, ladies," said a smooth voice from behind. Carole-Anne's eyes widened as she saw Derek smiling before them. To restrain herself from showing emotion, she grabbed on to Molly's hand and squeezed.

"Oh!" Molly gasped at the sharp pain in her hand. "Oh, how handsome you are," Molly said, trying to cover up her pain. "So dashing!"

Carole-Anne tightened her grip. "Ah! And manly!" Molly squealed.

"Uh, thanks, Sister Molly," Derek said. Put off by her strange behavior, he turned to Carole-Anne.

"How are you doing, Carole-Anne?"

Molly was sure she could hear her bones cracking. "Carole-Anne!" she shouted, causing both her and Derek to jump in fright. "Carole-Anne and I were just talking about how beautiful everything is and how happy we are for you both. Weren't we, Carole-Anne?" Molly subtly but harshly kicked Carole-Anne on her ankle.

"Ow! Oh yes, we were. We were actually just on our way to congratulate you two before you went to the reception."

Derek looked between the two women. "You won't be going to the reception?"

Carole-Anne apologetically shook her head. "I've got things at home I need to take care of."

"I see." Derek smiled. "Well. I'm glad I decided to come and talk to you right quick. I guess this is good-bye then."

"Good-bye?" Molly said with one eyebrow lifted.

"Yes, after the honeymoon, Stacy and I will be moving to California to work full time in the youth ministry. Today is pretty much our last day."

Molly looked at Carole-Anne who hid her heartache well enough, but Molly could tell everything inside of her was crumbling.

"Well, we'll miss you. But I'm sure you'll have more fun up in California," Molly said and glanced again at her friend. She was expressionless and didn't say a word. This was becoming awkward.

"We're very excited," Derek said, smiling. "I'm going to miss everyone here. But I know this is where the Lord wants me."

Derek finally cast his gaze at Carole-Anne who had yet to take her eyes off him.

"Carole-Anne, I, uh. I wanted to thank you."

"Thank me? For what?" she said, confused.

"For your honesty and for your love, though misplaced."

Carole-Anne opened her mouth, ready to take offense, but Molly lightly placed her hand on hers before her temper could rise.

"I guess what I'm really trying to say is not to give up on love. And that if you make Jesus your true love, then He will give you more than flesh ever could." Derek took Carole-Anne's hand and held it while looking in her eyes that began to moisten.

"He will bring you someone, someone to love you in the ways that you deserve to be loved. But all in His time."

Carole-Anne allowed the tears to fall and formed a weak smile on her lips. "Will you, uh," Carole-Anne struggled, "please forgive me for being such an idiot?" Derek laughed.

"It's better to be an idiot in love with Jesus than an idiot in love with another idiot." Derek shook Carole-Anne's hand and then shook Molly's'. After his short good-bye, he reunited with his bride and left to their reception.

Carole-Anne then turned to Molly and sighed.

"What?" Molly asked after Carole-Anne began to smile.

"I think Derek just called himself an idiot."

Molly thought back to the comment Derek made and was struck with laughter.

# *Life*

The day was beautiful. The backyard was full of flowers, and the air smelled of spring. It felt like the beginning of life, fresh and new. Leila had been with them for two months, and now that Paul and Katie had taken her in, it made life for Paul exciting. The new addition to their family was maybe exactly what they needed to pull his family out of depression.

When Leila came in to Paul's home, she was quiet and angry. She hardly spoke of her past and refused to answer any of Katie's questions. The first month in their home was frustrating, and Paul felt angry as well. He didn't know Leila and certainly didn't trust her. She was moody and had the mouth of a crocodile.

He wanted to kick her out so many times. She was so ungrateful. Paul had given her Michelle's old room, which tore his heart to pieces. But now, things were changing. Leila opened up to the boys and quickly became first their playmate, and now they saw her as their big sister. If his boys were happy with her, then maybe he should be too. It was easy to see that Leila had fallen in love with the two boys as well. Sometimes, Paul would awaken in the middle of the night and check on the boys and would find that they were not in their beds. When he would look into Leila's room, he would see them snuggled in her bed, her arms around both of them.

He watched as the boys ran around in the backyard chasing after Leila. She had changed so much. She was glowing now and looking more and more like a kid every day. Leila was so grown, but with the help of David and Michael, she was learning to be a kid again.

Oh, how Michelle would have loved to be outside with them on a day like this. She would have spent all day outside and would have dragged the entire family along with her. In a world where technology ran rampant, physical activity was almost taboo, but Michelle made it a point to be active in everything that she did. Paul saw the same trait in his niece.

"Hey, handsome," Katie said as she wrapped her arms around his waist.

"Hello, beautiful," Paul said, smiling.

"What are you doing?" Katie said, looking out the window into the yard.

"Watching the kids play."

Katie saw the warmth in Paul's eyes and embraced the warmth it gave herself. Though Katie herself came from a broken family, her own family became whole right before her eyes.

"It's amazing to see how much light Leila has brought into the house!" Paul said while bringing Katie close to him.

"Yes. She's changed so much. She was so grown up when she came here. So dry and empty. And now look at her. She's so active and alert. Like a real teenager."

Paul sighed and nodded.

"What's wrong?"

"I don't know. Leila seems happy enough now. But I feel like she's still holding all of the hurt inside. She refuses to go to church or to listen when we try to tell her of the Truth. I guess I just feel burdened. I know that Jesus is the only one who can really reach her, ya know? He's the only one who can set her free from her past."

Katie looked up at her husband and reached up and gave him a kiss. "What was that for?" Paul said, wrapping his arms around his wife.

"Does a wife need a reason to kiss her husband?" Katie said slyly.

"No." Paul laughed. "But I feel like there was a reason behind that kiss.

"Only that I love you. Just give her time, sweetheart. God brought her to us for a reason. The Lord will lead her to Him in

His own time and in His own way. All we can do is pray and be an example for her."

"You're right," Paul said, kissing his wife on the forehead. "You're always right." They stood in silence as they watched the boys tackle Leila to the ground. Paul looked down at Katie with mischief. Katie felt Paul's stare and looked up at him questioningly.

"What?" Katie asked slowly.

Paul smirked and leaned down to kiss his wife while he tenderly cupped her face.

"I was thinking Katie—"

"Uh-oh."

"It would be nice to add another addition to our family."

"What?" Katie yelled and drew back from Paul with shock written all over her face.

"Well, why not?" Paul laughed.

"Why not?" Katie repeated back.

"Can't you just see it? A new member to complete our growing family!"

"Oh, Paul, I don't think I'm ready for that."

"Why? We can have a boy, name him Roscoe. He can sleep in the backyard. He'll be a great playmate for the boys!"

Katie scoffed. "What?"

Paul laughed and lifted Katie up and swung her around.

"Paul, what's gotten into you?" Katie laughed.

"Let's get a dog. A big playful brown dog with a long tail!"

Paul kissed his wife and set her down. He didn't know why he never thought about it before. He loved dogs, and Katie liked dogs. Man's best friend would certainly do this family a lot of good.

"A dog?" Katie asked. "That's what you meant by another addition. A dog?"

"Sure, what else could I have meant?"

"I thought you were talking about a...a baby."

Paul's eyes widened. "A baby? You thought I meant a baby?"

"Well, yes, why do you think I freaked out?" Katie said, relieved.

Paul looked at his wife and took her hands in his and lifted her up in one quick swift and carried her up the stairs.

"Paul, you can't be serious!" Katie shrieked.

"Oh, I'm serious."

"What about the kids?" Katie whispered

"They're with Leila. They'll be fine."

The moment was beautiful with a riotous playful family downstairs, a loving husband whose first priority was no longer liquor; God had surely answered her prayers. They now had a full and happy family.

# *Fairy Tale*

"I don't want to go, Katie!" Leila shouted.

"Why?" Katie asked as she fixed her hair.

"Because it's stupid. I have no reason to go."

Katie laughed. "Honey, you have as much reason to go as I do. Come on now. It's only one service. What's really stopping you from going?"

"I don't know." Leila huffed and sat at the edge of Katie's bed. "Everything just seems so stupid."

"What does?"

"The whole idea of God. He isn't real."

Katie placed the last pin in her hair and sprayed it down with hairspray. After Katie was done, she stood in the doorway between her bathroom and her bedroom, looking at Leila.

"Are you sure about that, Leila?"

"As sure as I can be about anything. God isn't real. He's like Cinderella's fairy godmother or the tooth fairy. Face it, God is just another fairy from a fairy tale."

Katie sighed and walked over to her closet and disappeared within.

"Look, I'm sorry if I offend you. I just think God is a lie."

"Why a lie?" Katie said, hidden away in her walk-in closet.

"Because isn't he supposed to be like loving or whatever?"

"Yes."

"Well, if you ask me, I don't see anything loving about a God who lets a nine-year-old girl get abused by her father. I don't see the loving part when a little girl runs down the stairs after her father

91

shoots himself in the head in front of her, only to see her mother, her only source of happiness, sprawled out in a pool of blood. I don't see loving when a great family loses their daughter. Where's the love in that? Tell me!"

Leila shook with anger, and hot tears ran down her face. She hadn't meant to get all emotional, but there was nothing she could do about it now. She waited for a response from Katie.

Finally, Katie emerged from her closet, her eyes were red and moist with tears. Katie walked toward Leila and sat next to her, holding her hand firmly.

"I don't know why all those things happened, Leila. But I do know that everything happens for a purpose. These things, they make us stronger emotionally. And when we have a God who loves us to run to, it helps spiritually. The Bible says that Jesus is our comforter and our Helper. The memories of your past will always be there, but with Jesus on your side, your past won't hold you down. And right now, your past is keeping you down."

Leila shook her head. She would not be moved. she would not! Katie rubbed Leila's cheek. "Just one service, Leila. And if you don't like it, you don't have to go back."

Leila sighed. Why was it so important that she go to church? She knew that once people found out what she was, they would happily kick her out. And if they did, it would prove her in some way, right? There was no love and mercy when it came to God, and she would prove it to Katie.

"Fine. I'll go, but just this once."

Leila got up and went to her room to get ready. What did people wear to church anyway? She passed up a church one day on her way to a client, and all the ladies were wearing these funny-looking hats. She never saw Katie wearing a funny hat, and if she did, she hoped no one expected her to.

Leila didn't have any church clothes. She saw Paul and the boys wearing matching gray suits, and Katie was wearing a teal dress suit. They certainly took the phrase "Sunday best" to heart.

Leila rummaged through her drawers in her room and took out a pair of black pants. They were a little formfitting, but they would have to do. She brought out an off-white blouse and accented it with a diamond set. Leila was never a jewelry kind of girl, but the diamond set held a personal value to Leila. They once belonged to her mother. She wore them, hoping she would feel closer to her mother. But the diamonds weren't warm and inviting like her mother had been. They were cold and heavy. Come to think of it, her mother didn't wear jewelry that much. This was the last jewelry she could remember her mother wearing. She remembered how her father yelled at her mother one night.

"You're not leaving this house looking like a poor hag! You want everyone to think that I don't buy you nice things? You want everyone to feel sorry for you? You want everyone to tell you to leave me because I don't let you have nice things?"

"No, that's not it, Max! You know how I feel about jewelry!" her mother fought back. Leila didn't understand why her mother let her father hit her. Why didn't she just do what he said? She should have just put on the stupid necklace.

"I'm so tired of your stupid religion!" her father yelled and hit her again. This time, she fell to the floor.

Leila gasped and caught the attention of her father.

"Come here, Leila," he said with a gruff tone.

Leila slowly walked down the stairs clutching her tattered teddy bear.

Leila joined her father and looked down at her mother. Her father, dressed in a tux, looked dashing, but the anger in his eyes made him look ugly. Her mother was dressed in a beautiful long-sleeved silver gown. It was elegant and not too flashy. Her mother sat up, pressing her cheek where she was struck.

"Look at Mommy, Leila." Leila looked at her mother with confused eyes. Her heart ached as she saw tears streaming down her mother's face.

"Daddy, she's crying," Leila said, looking up at her father.

"Don't worry about that, Leila. Now don't you think Mommy would look beautiful if she wore that diamond set that Daddy bought her? Don't you think she would look pretty with earrings and a necklace that sparkled?"

Leila looked back at her mother and pictured the glittering jewels on her neck and ears. Leila smiled. "Mommy would look like a queen!"

"She would look like a queen, wouldn't she?" Her father said, squeezing her shoulders.

Leila's mother stood and let out a weak smile. "I would look like a queen, but I'm not a queen. I'm not treated like one either."

Leila felt her father tense up. She didn't know who to speak up for. She understood why her father wanted her mother to wear the jewelry; he just wanted her to look nice. But if her mother didn't want to wear the jewelry, then she shouldn't have to. She looked beautiful without them anyway.

"Daddy?" Leila tugged in her father's tux. "Mommy looks pretty without all the sparkly stuff. She still looks like a queen to me."

Leila's mother smiled down at her daughter, but her father just grew tenser.

"You've brainwashed her!" her father yelled. "You've turned her against me!" Leila was shoved to the floor and looked up with fear as her father began to take off his belt.

"No. Daddy, I'm sorry!"

Leila was then scooped up by her mother.

"Stop it, Max! Stop it!" Her mother yelled as Leila clung to her mother. whimpering.

"I'll put them on, all right? I promise I'll wear them tonight after I put Leila to bed. Okay?"

Max nodded out of breath. "Be quick. We're late."

Leila was put to bed. and her mother and father left to a banquet. Her mother left wearing the diamond set.

Leila was disrupted by her thoughts by a knock on the door.

"Come in," Leila said.

Michael peered through the doorway and smiled at Leila.

"Hey, little man!" Leila said warmly.

"Daddy sent me to see if you were ready." Leila looked at herself in her full-body mirror then turned to Michael. Leila spread out her arms and stood still.

"How do I look?" she said with a forced smile.

Michael placed his hand under his chin. "Hmm, you look nice, even if you're wearing pants."

"What's wrong with pants?" Leila said defensively.

"Women are not supposed to wear them."

"Well, why not?"

"Pants are for boys, not girls!"

Leila sighed. This was turning out to be a stressful morning.

"Okay, forget the pants. What else?"

Michael placed his hand under his chin again. "Those things on your ears."

"My earrings?"

"Yeah, and your necklace."

"You don't like them?"

"You look prettier without them," Michael said, smiling.

"I do?"

"Yeah, kind of like a princess. Daddy says a real princess doesn't need make up or fancy diamonds to make her pretty. Because she's pretty all on her own."

"Hmm." Leila brushed a hand over her diamond necklace.

"A princess, huh?"

Leila didn't believe in fairy tales, but when she left her room without the necklace and earrings, she walked out with her head held high and a confident smile. Just like she imagined a princess would.

# Love

Several days had passed since Derek's wedding, and to make sure Carole-Anne didn't get depressed, she kept herself busy. She studied scripture, visited Leila, authorized youth fellowships, made plans for ladies' fellowship, and read the book assigned by her book club. But when nighttime came and all the chores were done and all the church events were planned and scheduled, when the day was done and all she had were her thoughts, that's when her thoughts would bring her into despair.

Carole-Anne lay in bed and cried. She sobbed and clutched her Bible. Though she felt lonely, hurt, and betrayed, she knew she could rely on the comfort of the Lord Jesus Christ. She knew there was a reason for her brokenness and prayed for the will of God to be done in her life. She prayed for Leila that she would come to know the Lord soon, and she prayed for Paul and Katie to have patience and understanding. She prayed that God would heal her heart of pain, and she prayed that Derek and his wife were safe wherever they were. Finally, she slept. And when she awoke, she awoke with happiness that it was finally Sunday. Her joy escalated when Katie called her and said Leila would be joining them for morning service.

Carole-Anne scrambled through her Sunday-school notes and prayed over every page and for Leila who would hear them.

# *Life*

Paul pulled up to the church confident that Leila would feel at home. Grace Covenant Apostolic Church was a place where Paul and his family were able to worship and seek God fully. When Paul found himself in a place of hopelessness, he found a new hope in which could not be found in anything on Earth. He found complete peace in the arms of Jesus while the world continued in chaos.

He knew if the children of God embraced him here, then he knew Leila would be embraced as well. Paul prayed that Leila would feel comfortable and would realize that Jesus truly and deeply loved her.

As his family exited the car, he joined his wife, and they both silently prayed as they walked. Katie knew this to be a once-in-a-lifetime opportunity. If Leila did not enjoy the service, then it would most likely be her last.

Following close behind were the two boys and Leila who smiled lightly as the boys carried on about the wonders of Sunday school. Paul noted how silent Leila had been. She didn't say a word in the car, and though she smiled at Michael and David, she didn't say a word.

Paul sighed and squeezed Katie's hand lightly.

"It's going to be okay," Katie whispered.

"Should I be the one that's nervous?" Paul chuckled.

"It's a big step she's taking."

"I know God can handle it. He will handle it," Paul said, looking forward with determination as they entered Covenant Hills Apostolic Church.

# Fairy Tale

Leila sat hard and still on the pew in between Katie and the two boys. She sat in utter shock at all of the chaos. There was so much activity and energy that buzzed through the congregation. She was sure even the walls and floor beneath her feet trembled. The music was bold and loud. The singers where energetic and had this in-your-face attitude. The worship was bizarre. Some people clapped while others danced wildly, flinging their arms. Others rolled and leaped.

*This isn't a church. It's a circus!* Leila thought. Leila looked around at the congregation to see if anyone else was as shocked as she was. But to her surprise, no one else seemed bothered by the display. In fact, there was some who smiled and made whooping noises. She watched as the boys jumped and mimicked what they saw.

All these people seemed so joyful and outrageous in their worship. Leila thought church services were supposed to be quiet and reserved. She imagined people with their noses in the air, singing out of little books and a slow-speaking preacher who spoke on loving thy neighbor and then going home and beating their kids and cheating on their wives. At least that's what she was led to believe. But bottom line, church was boring and full of hypocrites. But this church was anything but boring!

The music vibrated, and the base added extra beats to Leila's heart, and the choir sang with such ferocity. Leila couldn't help but tap her foot and clap her hands. They sang loud, bold, and daring. But Leila didn't quite understand what they were singing about. Why did it excite and move her so? Leila then began to listen intently on the lyrics.

Holy Ghost! Lord I want that Holy Ghost fire!
It's what I desire most.
That precious Holy Ghost
Ain't gonna stop til I get it.
Reign down your presence.
I'm gonna dance until I get it
Sing until I feel it.
That Holy Ghost power,
Oh that sweet anointing.
The Holy Ghost is what I want most.

*Catchy,* Leila thought. *Catchy, but utterly confusing. What in the world is a holy ghost? What was so desirable about a ghost that's holy?* Leila couldn't begin to understand. But she knew it was something that she had to get to the bottom of.

# *Love*

Carole-Anne paced in her Sunday-school class. It wasn't long before that Katie called her and told her Leila would be coming to church this morning. Carole-Anne nearly jumped through the roof. She knew God was opening doors to this girl's heart so that through faith, she would know the heart of God and the power of His love.

The very thought gave Carole-Anne goose bumps. She was so excited and yet incredibly nervous. What if she said the wrong thing in her lesson? What if—no! She would not let doubt settle in her mind. She knew she was being led by Christ to minister to this girl. She knew the Lord favored Leila, and the fact that God had brought Leila to her meant that God had favored Carole-Anne as well. Carole-Anne stopped pacing and sighed. If God favored Carole-Anne, then that meant that God loved her. Tears formed in her eyes and a smile on her lips. She knew God loved her, which always went without saying. But it hit her; Jesus loved her, truly loved her. He suffered and died because he loved her. He rose again because He loved her, and He filled her with the Holy Ghost because He loved her. Here she was, looking for someone to love her when she had the love of the Savior all along.

"You're missing quite a worship service."

Carole-Anne turned around to see Molly smiling at her.

"Carole-Anne, you're crying!"

Molly went to her friend and touched her arm while her friend sobbed.

"Oh, Carole-Anne, what's wrong?" Molly asked, taking Carole-Anne and sitting her down.

"He loves me!" Carole-Anne sobbed.

"Who?" Molly asked.

"Jesus!"

Molly stared at Carole-Anne, "Yeah."

"No, you don't understand. He really really loves me!"

Molly laughed. "He sure does. Kinda thought you knew that."

"I did. But now, it's enough. His love is enough."

Understanding, Molly smiled. "Awe, Carole-Anne!" Molly embraced her friend and shed some tears as well.

"Ladies?"

Molly and Carole-Anne broke their embrace to see a concerned young man by the name of Matthew Graves.

"Is everything all right?" he asked.

"Yes," Molly said, sniffling. "Carole-Anne just realized that Jesus loves her."

"Molly!" Carole-Anne said, laughing.

Brother Matthew grabbed tissue for the two ladies and, smiling at Carole-Anne, said, "It's okay. Sometimes His love takes me by surprise too."

Carole-Anne laughed and wiped her tears while Molly blew her nose ferociously.

"Ew, Molly!"

"What? Like ya'll never do it?"

"So," Carole-Anne began, "what brings you to our Sunday-school class?"

"Oh, I thought someone would have told you. I'm supposed to sit today and watch you. Watch you give your lesson. Pastor said he would like me to take some responsibilities. I think he means for me to take Derek's place someday." He chuckled.

"You're going to be the new youth pastor?" Molly asked.

"No, no! Sister Molly. He just wanted me to watch how Sunday school goes and see if it's something I might like to be a part of one day," he responded

"Well, great!" Carole-Anne said, rising. "Well, welcome to our Sunday-school class," she said, spreading her arms. "Molly and I normally work together, but she's left me this year for the little ones," Carole-Anne said, poking out her bottom lip.

"Don't play that, I know you're just tickled as pie to be rid of me. Besides, the younger ones have a better sense of humor." Molly joked.

"Well, as long you're happy, Molly. I guess I'll have to settle for Brother Matthew," Carole-Anne said sarcastically.

Brother Matthew chuckled nervously.

"Why don't I show you around the room and get the feel of things before the kids come in?" Molly asked Brother Matthew.

"Oh, that'll be great." He chuckled

"Don't be so nervous, Matt!" Molly hit him reassuringly on the shoulder

"Oh, thanks, I guess I am a little nervous."

"Don't be." Carole-Anne smiled. "We have a great bunch of kids. You'll be fine."

Brother Matthew nodded and followed Molly around the classroom. Carole-Anne turned to a table on which her notebook rested. Pressing the notebook to her chest, she prayed silently for the lesson and for Brother Matthew and once again for Leila.

# *Life*

Paul looked over at his niece and met her eyes.

"Are you okay?" He mouthed.

Leila widened her eyes and nodded slowly. He knew she would be shocked at their worship. The poor girl had never been to a church service in her life, and her first experience would be something she would never forget.

The pastor came and took the microphone from one of the worship leaders and spoke into it, "Welcome to Covenant Hills Apostolic Church! Thank you for joining us this morning. Right now, the ushers are going to come and collect tithes and offerings. Please stand and greet one another. Children and youth are now dismissed for Sunday school. Parents, please take advantage of this growing ministry. The choir will sing as you give." The pastor then gave the microphone back to the worship leader, and the worship leader began to sing another song.

Paul looked over at Leila again and smiled.

"Do you want to go to Sunday school?" he asked her.

Before Leila could respond, Michael and David were in front of her, pulling her shirt.

"Please come, Leila!" Michael said.

"It's so much fun!" David chimed in.

"Yeah, we color and play dress up and Bible stories! I was Moses last time!" Michael said proudly

"Yeah, he had the beard and everything." David laughed.

Michael nodded up at Leila. "It itched," he admitted.

Leila laughed and looked at Paul and Katie with pleading eyes.

"All right, boys, you know Leila won't be in the same class as you. Come on, let's get going."

Katie got up and led the boys to the Sunday-school class while Leila followed behind.

# *Fairy Tale*

Leila walked into the Sunday-school class surprised to see it was full of teenagers. Each wall of the room was a different color, giving it a hip tone. The room was spacious and filled with abstract art. The furniture was impressive. There were orange couches, blue armchairs, and bright-green table chairs.

*Should a Sunday school look like this?* Leila thought Sunday school would be a little more structured like in the old days when the teachers would walk around with sticks and hit you when you got a scripture wrong. At least, that's what she was told.

"Leila!" a loud and happy voice said.

Leila turned to see Carole-Anne and sighed in relief. It was someone she knew!

"I'm so glad you came!" Carole-Anne said, hugging her.

Leila smiled and looked around at all the young people. She felt so intimidated in a room full of people her own age. How could she ever fit in? They all looked so normal and innocent like their biggest problem in life was their iPod got taken away. Leila felt so old compared to them. She wasn't a sheltered church kid. She knew what it was like to be beaten and raped, to sleep in her closet because it was the only place she felt safe. And that was just as a child.

As she got older, she knew the feeling of sleeping on the sidewalk, going from home to home, being passed from man to man. She experienced too much of the world to ever fit in with these kids or with these people. She hated to admit it, but the thought made her sad. She wasn't even considered a minor. Was she still considered a youth? Is this really where she belonged?

"Don't worry," Carole-Anne whispered in her ear, "everything's going to be fine."

Leila smiled. "We'll see."

Carole-Anne took Leila's arm and gave her a tour of the room starting with the game tables, the reading area, and what they called the Jesus Center.

"This is where we all sit and listen to the lesson. We call it the Jesus Center."

"The Jesus Center?" Leila repeated.

"Yeah, we call it that because Jesus is the center of our lives."

"Corny. Very corny," Leila said, laughing.

"Maybe, but it works," Carole-Anne said, smiling.

"I guess."

Leila followed Carole-Anne around and came across a woman with bright blonde hair and light-blue eyes.

"Molly," Carole-Anne began, "this is Leila."

"Oh my goodness!" Molly shouted and wrapped her arms around Leila. Leila tensed.

"I've heard so much about you!"

"Uh, thanks" Leila said, put off by Molly's strong Southern accent and energy.

"Don't worry," Carole-Anne said, placing her hand on Leila's shoulder, "you'll get used to Molly."

Leila laughed. "Yeah, it takes a whole minute to get used to me," Molly said, smiling.

Leila began to glance around the room as Molly and Carole-Anne continued in conversation. It wasn't long until Leila came upon a familiar face. He was tall, handsome, black hair, and clear blue eyes. Something about this man was incredibly familiar. She knew she'd seen him before.

"Carole-Anne? Who's that man over there?" she said, pointing to him.

"Oh, that's Brother Matthew. He's new to our church. I think the pastor wants to use him for some youth work. He'll be hanging around, watching the class today."

Leila stared, trying to place where she had seen him and when.

"Would you like me to introduce you?"

"Sure," Leila said, smiling.

Leila followed Carole-Anne as they made their way to the familiar man. She was almost positive she knew him. But from where? She knew no one from this church. She had no contacts except for her clients, who she no longer kept in contact with. Could it be? Leila's heart jumped at the thought.

"Brother Matthew," Carole-Anne said, smiling. "I want you to meet someone."

Leila couldn't help but feel smug. She wanted proof that church people were scum, and now she had her proof.

"Hello, Matthew," she said, smiling. The look on his face was priceless like a deer just before it gets run over. Leila laughed and shook her head.

"How pathetic!" she said, looking him over. He just stood like a statue, a stunned statue. "It's rude to stare," Leila whispered.

"I...I'm sorry. You two already know each other?" Carole-Anne asked confused.

"You could say he *knew* me," she said, smiling at the still stunned man. Carole-Anne looked at Leila and then looked at Brother Matthew, and she knew.

"So you are a church guy, huh? Sounds...exciting. So tell me, Matthew, what do you do in your spare time? Or is it too embarrassing to say?"

"Oookay! Leila, let me show you where you'll sit," Carole-Anne interrupted.

"No, don't bother." Leila stepped away from Carol-Anne. "I have nothing to learn here." Leila looked again at her former client. The shock was gone from his face, and all that remained was sorrow. Tears fell from his eyes as he walked away from the Sunday-school room.

For some reason, Leila had begun to feel guilty. But she pushed the guilt aside and angrily walked out of the classroom and went back to the main sanctuary and sat next to Katie with her arms folded.

"What happened? Are you okay?" Katie whispered.

"I don't want to talk about it," Leila said and slouched in her seat.

# *Love*

The phone rang and rang until finally, the voice machine picked up. "Hi, you've reached Matthew Graves. I'm not in, so leave a message, and I'll get back to you. Thanks and God bless."

"Matthew, it's Carole-Anne. Listen, I'm pretty worried about you. We haven't seen you at church. Please, just let us know if you're okay. We all love and miss you. I hope you call soon. Bye."

Carole-Anne hung up the phone and sighed. Four days had passed since the encounter between Leila and Brother Matthew, and both of them had discontinued any contact with anyone. According to Paul and Katie, Leila hadn't said a word since. She wouldn't accept Carole-Anne's calls. She hardly ate, and she refused to play with the boys. Paul and Katie were at a loss and so was Carole-Anne.

Of course, she was shocked when she realized that Brother Matthew had been Leila's client, but how were they to know?

He'd confessed to the church of his mistake, and the ministry took the proper action they felt necessary for it, but to do such an act with someone so young? How could he? Carole-Anne sat in her living room feeling frustrated and defeated. Did God send Leila here just to get confronted by her past? Did Brother Matthew repent and confess his sins just to have his past sins slap him in the face?

"Lord, I'm sure you know what you're doing, but the rest of us are walking around in the dark." She left the situation in His hands.

# *Life*

"For what is the hope for the hypocrite? Though he hath gained, when God taketh his soul? Will God hear his cry when trouble cometh upon him? Will he delight himself in the Almighty? Will he always call upon God? I will teach you by the hand of God; that which is with the Almighty will I not conceal" (Job 27:8).

As Paul read the words from Job, he thought of the situation that was present in their life. Of all the things Paul and his family faced—the death of Michelle, Paul's addiction to alcohol, and then opening their home to a street-wise orphan—so much had happened and was still happening.

Why didn't he think that Leila could have been the girl Brother Matthew fornicated with? He knew what Leila did for a living, how could he not think about Leila being the one who Brother Matthew had called to his house? He just didn't think—

*Be still.*

Paul fought the tears that threatened his eyes.

*How can I be still, Lord? Leila's so lost. We're all lost. I don't know what to do!*

*Be still.*

Paul sighed frustrated and angered.

*All right, Lord. All right, I'm leaving it in your hands.*

No sooner did Paul say those words did his doorbell ring. Paul jumped at the sound and tried to calm his racing heart as he walked to the door and opened it. Paul studied the visitor. He couldn't help but smile at the way the Lord worked.

# Fairy Tale

Leila dreamed the same dream. The mud, the stones that kept her trapped, and the man who set her free. Leila awoke to a tapping at her door.

"Leila?" the voice called.

"Mmm?" Leila groaned and turned to see the worried eyes of her aunt Katie.

"Leila, sweetie, will you get up?"

Leila loved how motherly Katie was. She was so very similar to her own mother.

"Do I have to?" Leila mumbled.

"Yes, honey. There's something we have to take care of as a family."

Leila quickly sat up and squirmed at the knot that had formed in her stomach.

"I'll be down in a minute."

Katie nodded and closed Leila's bedroom door.

The knot in Leila's stomach grew tighter, and fear gripped her throat in a tight embrace, making it impossible for her to breath. Her worst fear was coming true, and now all she knew how to do was run.

Leila jumped out of bed and grabbed her suitcase that lay under it. She always knew this day would come when she would cause so much trouble that Paul and Katie would decide it best if she leave. But she wouldn't give them that chance! She would leave before they kicked her out.

Leila frantically began throwing clothes inside her suitcase. Who was she to think it could last? She always knew there was something about her that was unlovable.

*That's right. You are unlovable. Who could ever love a used piece of trash like you?*

*But I don't do that anymore. I've changed!*

*You'll always be a toy to be used and tossed out.*

*No!*

*Yes. Run before you get tossed out again. Run!*

Leila closed the suitcase and lifted it as she headed for the door and opened it.

"Leila!" Katie said in surprise.

"Oh!" Leila screamed.

"What on earth are you doing up here?"

Leila fought the tears and the urge to wrap her arms around her aunt. Instead, she pushed passed Katie and said, "I'm leaving."

"Leaving? Leaving where?" Katie followed her down the stairs.

"I'm sorry I've caused so much trouble. I didn't...I didn't mean to. So I'm leaving." Leila began to walk but was pushed back. Katie had grabbed hold of Leila's suitcase.

"Now hold on a minute. You're not going anywhere."

Leila turned to Katie as tears stung her eyes. She wanted so much for Katie to be her mother. She wanted Paul to be her father and their boys to be her brothers. She wanted to be a part of the family. She wanted to be loved. And she thought for once she was. Leila collapsed on the stairs and buried her face in her hands and cried. Katie knelt beside her and tenderly rubbed her hair.

"Sweetie—"

"No! Don't mother me! You are not my mother! As much as I want you to be, you're not her! You will never be her! Ever!"

"Leila, I'm not trying to be her. But I am trying to understand. Why are you doing this?"

"I'm leaving before you kick me out."

Katie scoffed. "Kick you out?! We're not kicking you out!"

Leila's head shot up. "You're not?"

"No!" Katie laughed. "What would make you think such a thing?"

Leila paused, "Well, you said there was something that we needed to take care of, and I thought I caused so much trouble, that"—Leila's voice broke—"that you didn't want me."

"Oh, Leila." Katie wrapped Leila in her arms. "No, we would never do that. Never! You're part of the family, and family sticks together through the good times and the bad."

Leila sobbed. She didn't deserve to be loved like Katie and Paul loved her. Leila clung to Katie. How could this woman show her so much love and compassion after all that she'd done? Paul and Katie loved her as if she were their very own. She didn't understand, but she was so happy for it.

"Leila," Katie said, rubbing her forehead, "Paul and I never intended to love you like we do. But you brought such a light into our family just by being here and playing with our boys. You became part of the family. We're always going to be here for you."

Leila smiled. "I tried not to love you all. I tried so hard. I thought if I loved you, I would lose you."

Katie shook her head. "You could never get rid of us that easy."

Leila and Katie laughed and wrapped their arms around each other. Leila took in her scent, and she felt safe. For the first time since she came to live with her aunt and uncle, Leila uttered the words that made her feel pure and soft.

"I love you, Aunt Katie." Leila felt her aunt tense and then melt in her arms.

"I love you too, Leila."

Leila looked at her aunt's teary eyes and laughed. Leila wiped her aunt's tears as her aunt wiped hers, both laughing at their own emotions.

"Katie? Leila?" Paul said, carefully looking up at them. "Is everything all right?"

Katie stood and dabbed at her eyes. "Yes, baby, everything's okay. Leila and I were just having a little girl talk."

Leila stood and looked down at her uncle. He had been like a father to her—the father she never had. Leila walked down to him and leapt into his arms.

"Whoa!" Paul gripped her and, with surprise, looked up at his wife who smiled brightly.

"I love you, Uncle Paul."

She had felt the same reaction when she had told Katie. Paul tensed and then melted in her arms.

"Oh, Leila. I...I love you too." Paul squeezed Leila tighter, savoring the moment. It was until a cough was heard from the living room did Paul put Leila down.

"Leila," Paul said, rubbing her shoulders, "there are some people here to see you."

"Me?" Leila wondered. Leila walked over to the living room and stopped in shock when she saw the tall, dark-haired man with the clear-blue eyes. His hair was unkempt, and his face seemed hidden by his five-o'clock shadow. And sitting across from him was the woman who saved her life.

"Carole-Anne!" Leila ran to her friend who met her and wrapped her arms around her.

"Carole-Anne, I'm sorry. I'm so sorry I didn't mean to cause all this trouble."

"It's okay. It's okay. That's why we're here—to talk about it."

Leila looked at the man who sat on a single chair across the room. His face seemed hardened by a lack of sleep and a five-o'clock shadow.

"Hello, Leila," he said gruffly. His voice sounded so hard and heavy. Leila's heart sank in to her stomach, and tears dropped from her eyes.

"Hi, Matt," she said, finally. Paul and Katie walked in and sat on the couch with Carole-Anne and left a spot in between Katie and Carole-Anne and motioned for her to sit.

"I think it's time," Matthew began, "that we talk some things out."

Leila held her aunt and Carole-Anne's hand. She knew now that with her friends and family by her side, she could face the demons from her past.

"Okay," Leila said, nodding her head.

"Okay," Matthew said, rubbing his hands together.

"I'm sorry," Leila blurted. "I'm sorry for calling you out in front of everybody. That was uncalled for. I just felt so good about proving my point."

"What point was that?" Katie asked.

"That all church people were fake. But once I realized who you were," she said, talking to Matthew, "and after I said those awful things to you and I saw the look on your face, I realized that you weren't upset with me or even embarrassed but sad. I actually felt bad for making you sad."

Matthew nodded. "I wasn't sad because of what happened. I was sad because I felt like I ruined the only chance you had at knowing God. I was never mad at you, Leila. I was mad at myself for causing you to run away. I know what it's like to be so close and yet so far away. And once again, I had ruined everything. I ruined my chances of escaping my past, and I felt like I ruined all your chances to escape yours."

Leila sat silently. "But you didn't make me run away. After all that stuff happened, I locked myself away. I slept mostly, and every time I fell asleep, I would have the same dream over and over again. I dreamt that I was covered in dirt, and the dirt became so heavy that I fell to the floor, and the dirt formed clumps of stone at my hands and feet. But then this man showed up in a white robe. I couldn't see his face. But his hands and feet were scarred. And he touched my head, and when he did this, the stones fell apart, and the dirt disappeared. I was clean. I've had this dream almost every night even before I ever met Carole-Anne. When I asked the man who he was, he said his name was Jesus, the only name under heaven and earth. So you see, I couldn't run away, 'cuz this guy Jesus kept following me around."

Everyone sat in silence. "I never believed in God, but now I'm not sure." Leila sighed.

Carole-Anne squeezed Leila's hand. "Leila, that Sunday you came to church, I wrote a lesson for Sunday school. I've talked it over with your aunt and uncle and Brother Matthew, and I think we should bring this up."

"Okay."

"But first," Brother Matthew interrupted,

"Leila, I need to apologize to you. I was wrong in doing what I did. And I know it'll be hard to see me as the man I am striving to be, instead of the man who...," Matthew's voice broke and buried his face in his hands.

Leila got up and held his hand. "It's okay. I forgive you, Matt. Will you forgive me?"

Matthew looked at Leila and put his hand over hers. "I already have." Leila smiled and placed a hand on his shoulder and then walked back to her seat.

Carole-Anne began, "I know you're very new to the Bible. So to help you, I've brought you your very own Bible."

Leila reached over and received the leather-bound Bible. Her name was engraved in gold.

"Wow. It's beautiful."

"Look in the back," Katie pointed out. "This'll help you when you study it." Katie opened her Bible and ran her finger through the concordance.

"This is great. I've never actually read the Bible. I only know what people have told me. And what I've been told hasn't been very good."

"Well, that's why we're here," Paul said, smiling. "To help you and to help each other learn all we can about God."

"That sounds really great and all, but I'm pretty sure there's no plan of salvation for someone like me."

Matthew rubbed his hands through his hair. "If there's hope for me, then there's certainly hope for you. God is already reaching out to you through these dreams. And He'll do so much more when you study His word. He'll speak to you in ways that will make you realize how precious you are in His sight."

"Leila," Carole-Anne continued, "in this Bible are many stories of how God speaks to His people. In here you'll find all the ways that God loves us, and for many people, they devoted their lives to Him because He loved them, and God proved his love. But for many, His love was not enough. I want to tell you about the story of Hosea. I was going to teach on Hosea at Sunday school. Will you allow us to tell you the story now?"

Leila looked around at the people around her. She had grown to trust them. Even Matthew—he was a man who made mistakes, but instead of throwing the blame on someone else for his mistakes, he took responsibility for them. He owned up to them, and now was trying to make it right.

"Okay, tell me the story."

The attention was then aimed at Carole-Anne. Her countenance had changed. Leila saw the same urgency in Carole-Anne that she had seen in her mother many years ago.

"Hosea was a prophet, um, a man who speaks for God. One day, God told Hosea to marry a woman, a woman who would not have been known in good society. The Bible describes her as a woman of whoredoms. This was a woman who knew many men and would continue in fornications even when married."

"Like me?" Leila said, hurt.

"Like you used to be," Katie said, squeezing her hand.

"By asking Hosea to marry this woman, God illustrated how He felt for Israel. God loves us as if we were his bride, and he was our husband. He wanted Hosea's wife, Gomer, to illustrate how the people strayed away from Him. Hosea loved Gomer, but Gomer did not love Hosea, and at some point, Gomer left Hosea to be with other men."

"So what were God's people running to? What were they doing that caused them to stray away from God?" Leila asked.

"They were worshipping other gods. The Bible says that God is a jealous God and that He is the only God. But I also believe that even though they worshipped other false gods, the people also allowed other things like wealth to get in the way of their worship to God."

"That happens a lot today." Paul nodded. "Even in my own life. When our daughter died, instead of turning to God, I turned to the bottle. In a way, that bottle became my god. It took the pain of my children and the faithfulness of my wife to help me realize what I was turning into. But God restored me. He forgave me. He took me back just like Hosea took Gomer back."

"God is always faithful to us," Matthew began. "We may not always be faithful to Him, but He is faithful to us. He is a God of judgment, and He's a God of mercy."

"So, okay, I get it. God loves me, but then if He loves me, why did I go through all the things I went through? God is here for me now, but where was he when I needed him the most?"

The attention was then brought to Katie. It seemed like no one was quite prepared to answer that question, but Katie seemed cool and collected.

"Your mom," Katie began, "loved God, but she allowed her love for a man to interfere. But eventually, her love grew and grew despite her situation. She was able to share with you the story of Jesus. She taught you how to call on him."

"A lot of good that did." Leila rolled her eyes.

"In the end, your mom died loving Him, and I'm sure she would be so proud to know that you are on your way to know Him. God allows things to happen because He wants to use us. I believe Michelle passed away so that we could carry on the hope of His word. Imagine if we had not had God when Michelle passed? Imagine if we were lost in the world with no hope of a heaven or God. Life would have been unbearable. It was because of God that we were able to overcome, and now we can tell people that. It was God that saved us, and it was God that saved you from a life of sin. And now you're here to help the hundreds of people out there that share your past. We are now equipped with the experience we need to help all the lost souls out there. God wants to use you and your story."

"Me? He wants to use me?"

"All these years, men have used and abused you. But now God wants to use you to lift yourself up. He loves you and sees you as a precious jewel."

Throughout the night, each person took a turn to help Leila understand the many ways that God loved her. She listened intently as the night went on. As each person spoke, she felt closer and closer to this unseen God. Finally, a decision had to be made, and the decision for Leila was a no-brainer.

"I want to be baptized."

# Love, Life, and Fairy Tale

*2 years later*

The man spoke with a passion so deep and moving that if a single pin dropped, it would have been heard throughout the entire congregation. Carole-Anne shook her head in awe as she watched the man of God speak to the congregation of the power of God's love.

"Carole-Anne?" called the bundle of fumbling white. Carole-Anne laughed at the site.

"I can't—I can't find the sleeves or where my head is supposed to go. Help!" Carole-Anne walked over and pulled out a sleeve and then the other, which was promptly followed by arms, and then popped out Leila's head.

"Oh!" Leila gasped. "I can breathe!"

Carole-Anne took a moment to study Leila's appearance.

"Well?" Leila said, holding out her arms, "How do I look?"

"Beautiful," Carole-Anne said.

Leila smiled and turned to face the mirror. "Ugh, more like a snowball. I look ridiculous!" Leila said, smoothing out the wrinkles she had made in her gown.

Carole-Anne shook her head.

"No. You look wonderful."

Leila smiled and studied herself in the mirror.

"It's time, Leila. Are you ready?"

Leila turned from the mirror with her chin lifted. "Yes. I'm ready."

Katie and Paul entered her dressing room and fawned over the blushing bride.

"Leila, you look gorgeous!" Katie reached over and hugged her niece, allowing tears to flow.

"Thanks, auntie." She blushed

"Oh, your mom would be so proud of you."

"I wish she could be here." She said fighting the tears.

"I know she would want to be."

"Uncle Paul"—Leila reached over to her uncle—"you're not tearing up, are you?"

"Who me? No, it's this boutonniere stirring up my allergies." Paul wiped away tears and cleared his throat. "There, all better." He laughed.

Paul embraced his niece and looked her over. She was the perfect bride, and her dress was modest and sleek. He was so proud. He imagined this is how his daughter might have looked when she got married. And now at twenty and still innocent despite her troubled life, he had the pleasure of walking his niece, his adopted daughter down the aisle for the next phase of her life.

As the wedding party got themselves ready, Leila breathed in deeply, allowing the scent of her roses to relax her. As her party began to walk down the aisle, she clenched to her uncle's arm.

"Don't worry, you look wonderful."

Leila chuckled lightly and tried to control her breathing. She was a bride in white. White meant purity. Her past was anything but pure. But now God made her white as snow. The wedding march began, and she lifted her head up high and was escorted down the aisle. The crowd smiled, and some wept, but her gaze was toward her groom. He stood so tall and confident. His eyes were locked on his bride.

Matthew gazed at his bride. He smiled and chuckled to himself. How could he be so lucky? Who would have ever thought that Leila and he would end up this way? She had grown so much. Right before his eyes, she became a woman after God's own heart, and she had owned his heart.

Paul led his niece to her groom, kissed her hand, and brought their hands together.

As the ceremony began, Paul and Katie sat hand in hand with tears streaming down their cheeks. How amazing God was! He had restored their family. Paul looked at his wife and placed his hand on her stomach. It was firm under his touch. Katie smiled and placed her hand over her husband's. They were completely overjoyed over this new addition that would soon enter their family. God had taken a family completely shattered by a tragedy and restored and blessed them.

Carol-Anne stood next to Leila, amazed at how God has worked. Her heart rejoiced in the Lord. As someone who's greatest desire was to be loved, she now accepted the love of God and that sacrificial love was enough. *God, if all I have is you for the rest of my life, it will be such a blessed life!*

Leila stood hand in hand with her groom. She couldn't believe where God had brought her from. From promiscuity to a woman who yearned to please God and now will live to please her husband. Love and God were nothing but myth and fairy tale, and now God and the love of her husband were the only truths in her life.

"I now pronounce you husband and wife. You may kiss the bride."

Together, Matthew and Leila grew in the Lord, bonded in their love and faith. Together, they began a work with troubled youth. They led seminars and shared their story. As a reminder of the power of God's love and grace, they named their first son Hosea. It was later prophesied that he too would be used mightily of the Lord. Leila prayed for all those who walked a path in darkness. She prayed for the generation that would come after her. She prayed fervently that love and life would be seen as though from God, a gift and not a curse. She prayed continually that the truth of the one and only God would not continue to be fantasy to an unbelieving world but a truth worth life and love itself. She knew life would continue in hardships, and love could end in brokenness, but with, God there would always be happily ever after, and in her faith, that is exactly how she lived— happily ever after.

# About the Author

Vickie Valladares has spent most of her life with her nose in a book or hands busy with writing. She was raised with amazing stories of how God moved in her life at birth and through her mother. Born four months premature with no hope for survival, Vickie's mother received a word from God that He would spare her child. Once Vickie was born, her mother would tell her stories of how she saw God himself standing over her incubator, His hand covering her tiny body and telling her mom that their child would be fine. Within six months, Vickie was able to go home and has lived a normal healthy life.

At the age of fifteen, Vickie recommitted her life to Jesus after having a Holy Ghost experience at a Pentecostal church. From then on, she worked hard in her writing and learning all she could about His word. At the age of twenty, her mother passed away from lung disease. The tragedy left her faith shaken and her heart broken. Two years after her mother's death, she had started to feel the urge to write again. She finished her manuscript that she started when she was nineteen and began writing skits and poems for her church. She now lives in Killeen, Texas, with her husband Jack and Boston Terrier, Roscoe, and attends New Life Apostolic Church.